MOANA,
Hope you enjoy
my story!

Contents

Acknowledgments

I can confidently say that all of my friends and family in some way, shape, or form helped to make this happen, and I send my gratitude to each and every one of you in my incredible community across the globe. Your friendships and love have supported me through the highest highs and lowest lows, and I'm forever grateful to all of you. I want to highlight a few people who specifically helped in the actual process of writing and publishing my book and empowered me to complete this creative journey.

First and foremost, I thank my wife Brita who has stuck with me from the beginning, endured every horror of this injury and recovery with me, and has never for one second flinched in her support and commitment to me. You listened to me brainstorm each chapter, read and revised and helped me remember important details, and always had faith in me to pursue this endeavor.

From the bottom of my heart, I thank my parents Minoo and Shahin, from whom I have learned valuable lessons throughout my life and continue to learn from every single day. I'm honored to know I've inherited your strength, love, passion, and dedication to life, all qualities that were essential to the publication of this book.

I want to thank my editor Jude Berman who patiently worked with me through every step of this process and enabled me to transform, elevate, and improve my writing dramatically from when I started this project. Every time I thought a chapter was done, she pushed me further and encouraged me to go back in, revise again, and make it even better.

I'm grateful for all the readers of my blog over the last five years. The idea of writing this book was initiated by your comments and feedback to my posts. If I hadn't known that my perspectives and stories were interesting and impactful to you, I would have not have taken on the monumental task of writing this memoir. Consider yourselves my first draft editors and reviewers.

I owe a special thanks to David Nihill who apart from being an incredibly supportive friend, has basically acted as my book consultant, advisor, and literary agent all in one. Navigating the book writing, publishing, and marketing process is incredibly difficult, but I had a secret weapon in David who had numerous conversations with me, offered endless amounts of advice, and on whom I could always count for honest and helpful insight.

Thank you.

Introduction

I didn't want to write this book. I really didn't.

I never expected to have my entire life turned upside down, experience a devastating injury, or abandon a body that had always been great to me. Although the early years of my childhood were filled with unpredictability and consistent change, the first three decades of my life were pretty incredible. I always had a supportive and loving family who gave me every opportunity to succeed.

I was born in Iran, but left as an infant when my parents decided to escape a difficult political climate and seek a better life elsewhere. This resulted in a six-year journey across the planet, taking me to four different countries and a dozen different housing situations. I learned three languages as a child. By the time we moved to California, I was seven-years-old and no stranger to new experiences and big life changes. Adapting to new countries, cities, languages, communities, schools, and friends had become just another part of my childhood, and I assumed it would prepare me to encounter practically any significant life change in the future.

My parents instilled a love of nature and the outdoors in me from a young age. Camping in Yosemite and the Sierras of California, swimming in Lake Tahoe, and going on Sunday bike rides with my father were unforgettable experiences that shaped my pursuits as an adult. This love of nature—combined with me attempting to play every sport under the sun—created a deep love for athletics and physical activity. It also cultivated in me a profound respect for the incredible opportunities good health could afford. As such, I maintained a commitment to remain physically active throughout my life. Travelling the world, enjoying nature, achieving athletic accomplishments, and living a healthy life were all made possible by a consistent appreciation for my body's abilities.

And then, in one instant… it all changed.

Yes, it sounds cliché, but there's no other way to describe it. What started out as an ordinary summer Saturday turned into an infamous night I will never forget, and whose impact I will never escape.

I didn't know a thing about spinal cord injury before I woke up immobile in the hospital and was told I was very lucky to be alive. The doctors showed me X-rays of my broken spine, and of the vertebrae in my neck, which had exploded into tiny pieces. They explained that due to the severe impact to my spinal cord, the damage was irreversible. My life would never be the same. They said I had lost many functions in my body that I would never regain; that the finality of the injury was inevitable and unchangeable. And they told me that the best thing I could do was to accept and adapt to my new reality as quickly and wholeheartedly as possible. The body I had known, enjoyed, worshipped, and taken great care of, was now—literally and figuratively—broken.

One of the most devastating aspects of a spinal cord injury is the unpredictability of the person's ability to recover. Truly, no two injuries are the same. I've met dozens of people who broke the same vertebrae in their neck as I did, and they all have their own unique physical limitations and wildly varying levels of function, or lack thereof. The unifying theme I noticed for all these people is the negativity and pessimism they encountered with medical staff, especially in the prognosis and initial stages of their recovery. Neither the quality of care, nor the specific insurance provider, nor the geographic location of the injury and ensuing care seems to matter when it comes to the medical establishment's approach to spinal cord injury recovery.

The common attitude among most surgeons, doctors, and neurological experts is that once the spinal cord has been injured, the damage is done and the expectations for healing are slim to none. Moreover, the prevalent—if not ubiquitous—thinking is that whatever healing *might* occur will conclude within six months or a year; two years if you're lucky. Therefore, those of us who suffer a spinal cord injury find ourselves faced with a ticking time clock that only makes recovery more challenging and anxiety producing.

I always assumed that living in a wealthy country, with leading research institutions and access to medical innovations and technological breakthroughs, would ensure a nuanced and sophisticated approach to any medical condition or injury. It was a rude awakening to be told by medical personnel with great conviction and certainty what my body would be able—and more significantly, *unable*—to do in the future. The time frame I was given for my recovery seemed surprisingly arbitrary, and I began to question it. Why would my body stop trying to repair and improve itself after a year? Couldn't other factors, such as my overall health and my commitment to improve influence the projected potential for recovery? What about alternative approaches or treatments? Why did there have to be a prognosis at all; why couldn't doctors embrace the inherent ambiguity of the situation and simply admit they did not know?

Early on after my injury, these questions plagued me. I was infuriated by the widespread negativity I encountered from so-called experts. I began speaking to other people with spinal cord injuries to see if they shared that experience. Two friends—one an experienced researcher—helped me create a comprehensive survey, which I sent to as many people with spinal cord injuries as I could find, all across the country and even some internationally. After reading the sixty-three survey responses and recounting the numerous conversations I had with people in-person, I realized that virtually all had dealt with the same negative attitude. They had been persuaded to reduce—if not eliminate—their expectations and tame their desire for a significantly improved quality of life.

This confirmed to me that committing to my recovery was about more than just my physical condition and how much or little I could improve. It was about challenging a prevailing way of thinking that was extinguishing hope for the people who, in their most vulnerable time, needed it most. It broke my heart to be given so little encouragement at the prospect of regaining function in my body, and it broke my heart again every time I heard someone tell me the same thing. So I embarked on my journey to seek answers to my lingering questions, to explore the true potential of my body's capabilities, and to break beyond the limits and boundaries that had been imposed upon me.

***

Life after a devastating injury is complicated and eventful, to say the least. I am often overwhelmed when I look back on my experiences, especially those in the initial months after my injury: interactions with doctors and medical professionals, conversations with family and friends, solitary moments contemplating my situation, the breakthroughs and the setbacks, the discoveries about an unfamiliar body, and the daily fight to survive and slowly put back together the pieces of my life.

From the beginning, I recognized the significance of every step along my path of recovery. Beginning during my first days in the hospital, I took meticulous notes of not just my experience and daily activities, but also of my deepest feelings, fears, thoughts, and expectations at each moment. My family took videos and photos of every hospital room and each physical therapy gym. Even when I did not yet have the strength or hand function to write or type, I recorded video journals and audio notes. I started writing a blog four months after my injury, in which I shared the details of my experience. I continue to write my blog to this day.

I used many of my recorded memories to help me write this book— although some of the videos are still too painful for me to watch. In fact, many of my memories seem surreal and dreamlike now, as if I could not possibly have lived through them. While I am grateful to have so many detailed recollections, many of them don't seem interesting to me anymore. More importantly, many would likely not be interesting to you, the reader. For this reason, although my book follows a chronological path, I have chosen not to focus on a sequential retelling of the details of each and every week or month following my injury. Instead, I focus on the moments, interactions, breakthroughs, challenges, and triumphs that capture the essence of my journey.

Each chapter explores one part of my complicated road to recovery as I seek to achieve what I was told was unachievable. I commit myself immediately to the ultimate goal of getting back on my feet and to doing everything in my power to work toward that goal. Yet, the implications of my injury extend beyond my own experience. Every chapter illustrates how encountering the unexpected—and finding ways to move forward—

affects my family, friends, and loved ones. I offer these lessons because I believe they will resonate with readers who face a similar journey.

I have changed the names of some individuals and identifying details in their stories in an effort to maintain privacy, but everything else I share is accurate and genuine. My intention is not to take a devastating situation and paint it in a positive light for the sake of appearing happy or inspiring you through platitudes or falsehoods. Neither do I want to systematically describe the suffering, misery, and adversity I went through and chronicle the reasons a life-changing injury is so difficult and disheartening. There are plenty of other memoirs with such narratives. Rather, my intention is to share my honest account of a situation no one expects to encounter: having life transformed in one split second; dealing with the repercussions that follow; and navigating through life with an entirely different body, mind, and perspective.

I hope you enjoy my story.

1.

An Operation, a Sponge, and a Very Long Night

It's 7 pm, and the surgery is over. I've been carved up like a jack-o-lantern, had my spine completely reconstructed, and am just now waking up in bed and remembering when this all started.

It was a few minutes before noon when the nurse tilted her head in the doorway and made the announcement: "The surgeon is ready. It's time to go, Arash." And with that, this strangest of transformations of my body began. I was already losing consciousness as they rolled me down a series of hallways, on the same ICU bed I had inhabited since arriving in the frenzied ambulance two days earlier.

I have no idea what they did to me for those seven hours, no conception of what my body endured in an operation in which I was told there was a real possibility of serious complications, even death. I didn't comprehend the strength of the anesthetics, of the medications they used to keep me unconscious and numb, yet alive. They sliced open my body just inches below my brain and went to work, painstakingly repairing what had been injured in less than a second during my three-story fall onto concrete—a result of being locked out of a friend's apartment and deciding to try to climb in through the balcony and save the day.

I never got a preview of the titanium rods and screws before they were drilled into my damaged spine, allowing me to have a functional neck again, and promising to remain a part of my physiology for the rest of my life. Ultimately, I didn't have a choice. For all of human history, until just a couple of decades earlier, a spinal cord injury such as mine would have resulted in death if not in the first few hours after the injury, then within days or weeks.

The room is unusually empty when I first open my eyes. I'm holding the trusty red squeeze ball in my right hand, and the metal halo on my head has been replaced with a cumbersome brace surrounding my entire neck, stabilizing my head from my ears down to my sternum. I can see the various screens and monitors in my peripheral vision, beeping and flashing, with straight lines and curved, dancing up and down across a blue background, relaying numbers unfamiliar to me but critical to my survival.

I can hear the muddled conversations of my parents in an adjoining room as they talk to the nurses and medical staff. I know they're talking about the surgery, restating and explaining the steps, like coaches reviewing a game, analyzing their players' strengths and shortcomings. The surgeon, Dr. Chang, is answering their questions now, speaking softly but with great confidence. Although they're out of my sight, I can sense my parents' hesitant nods. I can imagine their fear-stricken faces as they hear the details of the operation.

My mouth is dry. Extremely, inexplicably, painfully dry.

I glance around the room a few times, trying to fight my way through the haze created by all the medication that's flowing through my body, and then they all walk in together. The surgeon stands to my left, my parents are just behind him, and the assistants look on from the foot of my bed.

Dr. Chang says, "The surgery went very well, Arash. It took a while, but everything went smoothly."

Because I feel like I've been hit by an eighteen-wheeler and can barely move any part of my body, it's difficult to comprehend what this means.

Dr. Chang acknowledges my silence and continues. "We had to go in from both the front and back of your neck. Before we could rebuild your spine, we had to clean out all the small pieces of broken bone. After we finished in the front, we made a larger incision in the back of your neck and fused together your two broken vertebrae with the healthy vertebrae above and below. So you have titanium rods stabilizing your neck from C4 through C7. As I said, it was a time-consuming process and took us a little longer than expected, but I'm happy with the results."

This moment, like all others during my time in the ICU, feels completely surreal. We can't be talking about *my* neck, can we? It isn't *my* body strapped to a bed, unable to move? This entire conversation about broken vertebrae and titanium rods couldn't possibly apply to *me*. There is no way any of this is happening, right?

I want to scream at Dr. Chang, plead my case and tell him he's got the wrong person. I'm the guy who was standing on a 12,000-foot mountain six days ago, with a fifty-pound backpack loaded with extra food to help out my friends who couldn't carry as much. I'm the guy who bikes all over the city! Who stuffs his backpack with groceries, rides his bike up a steep San Francisco hill, and then carries everything up the three flights of stairs to his apartment. This whole broken neck thing can't be about me. Now just snap me out of this nightmare, Dr. Chang, and let me get back to my life!

I close my eyes and hope and pray and wish that when I reopen them I'll be back in my own bed, looking out the bay windows of my bedroom, seeing the Victorians of the Haight-Ashbury and the tall, swaying trees of Golden Gate Park in the distance. I think of the tricks I've used to get out of bad dreams in the past: suddenly snapping my head backwards, shifting my glance quickly around my surroundings, trying to run really fast. But none of them give me results now. I open my eyes.

The nightmare continues, and I'm forced to acknowledge the gravity of my situation, to reluctantly accept that this may actually be my existence. I'm suddenly well aware of where I am. The ICU room is still here. My parents, with their swollen, devastated faces, are here, too, desperately trying to hold back their tears. I battle through the numbing fog of the medication and try to comprehend exactly what's going on.

I finally ask the question most dominant on my mind: "Dr. Chang, will I walk again?"

I half expect Dr. Chang will laugh me off, throw his arm around my shoulder, and insist that I'm crazy to be so worried, that I've seen too many movies, that the surgery seems to have given me an unexplainable penchant for being overly dramatic. I assume he will be flabbergasted by the ridiculousness of my question and remind me that it's an injury, and that like all injuries, it will improve, and I will inevitably recover. He will chastise me and ask what the hell is wrong with me for thinking such inexcusably illogical thoughts.

He sighs. There's no laughter, no backslapping reassurance that "everything is going to be okay," no asking why I would ask such a silly and unreasonable question. His eyes glance away for a split second, seemingly searching for a way to lessen the blow, and when they land back on me, he sighs a second time, more heavily.

"Well, it's tough to say exactly what will happen, and I can't say about if or when walking may happen, but I think… you may have… a chance of… some kind of recovery."

He sees the shock and dismay in my face, evident despite the heavy anesthetics still in effect, and he continues: "Look, the spinal cord heals unbelievably slowly. Some people say a centimeter per month, others say slower. You broke your neck, so imagine how long your spinal cord will have to heal before it gets all the way to the bottom."

He can tell I'm doing the calculations in my head, quickly estimating the number of inches from the base of my skull to my tailbone, dividing that to get the centimeters, then adding up the months. I end up with thirty-five, just shy of three years.

Before I can contemplate how horrifically long that is, he keeps talking. "It's hard to predict how or what kind of healing you'll get. You just have to… you know… try to stay positive. And hope for the best."

That's it. In that instant, my life has been turned upside down. Everything I've ever known about my body, my abilities, my career, and my ambitions is out the window, and replaced with… what? With the assurance that I have a chance at "some kind of recovery?" Or with the fact that the nurses are already referring to me in terms of my physical impairment? Or with the knowledge that I won't be going back to work this week, that I won't finish packing up my room in preparation for my much-anticipated move into a new apartment?

The effects from the medication are suddenly overwhelming, preventing me from processing my situation with clarity or integrity.

And so I drift off, half asleep, half bewildered that I still haven't woken up from this terrible nightmare.

***

I open my eyes.

It's almost dark outside, the final slivers of color from a long-lingering summer sun are still streaking the sky, and the room is quiet. I immediately know I was given another dose of morphine because my entire body feels like it's floating and my senses are jumbled together into a single, artificially serene, flowing mess of numbness.

My mother enters the room, sees that I'm awake, and quickly comes to my side and holds my hand. "Are you feeling okay?" she asks.

"I'm not sure I know how I'm feeling, Mom."

She swallows hard, looks down at the ground, then back up at me. Her eyes are red and sunken, the skin on her face barely dry from the consistent, almost clockwork bouts of crying I can tell she's endured since she showed up at the hospital in a panic three nights earlier. What I put her through is every parent's worst nightmare: to be woken up at 3 am by a ringing phone, told that your child—your only child in her case—is in critical condition at the hospital and you need to come immediately. But I'm still reeling from the earlier conversation with Dr. Chang, so I can't allow in the flood of guilt, embarrassment, and shame I otherwise would be feeling.

"Mom, what am I gonna do?"

"Well, they said they have to keep you here for a few more days, and then…"

"No, Mom," I interrupt her. "I mean, what am I gonna *do*? You heard what he said about walking, about this injury. Is this for real? He didn't exactly portray confidence when it came to my recovery. This can't be happening!"

She squeezes my hand harder and sighs patiently. I can sense her doing her best to fight off the tightening in her throat and the beginning of another round of tears. Yet in those red, swollen eyes, I can also see a familiar surge of strength, dedication, and resilience—qualities that allowed her to make her way out of a small, rural town in Iran; learn three languages at an academic level; earn her PhD; and become a successful professor at UC Berkeley.

"Well, I'm not sure," she responds. "You've worked so hard your entire life to keep your body in great condition. You don't just rely on your physical capabilities, you enjoy them. Think of what you've done in your life and all the places you've traveled to, and the trails you've hiked, and all of the exploring you've done. You've accomplished a lot physically, more than most people do in a lifetime. Maybe now you have to think about relying a little less on your physical pursuits, and transition to more mental pursuits, ways you can use your brain and not necessarily your body."

At first her words sound insensitive and conciliatory, as if she's dismissing any future possibilities for my physical abilities, but I know her intentions are as loving and positive as they always have been. At no point in my life, not even for a blink of an eye, has my mother been discouraging or doubting of my potential to do anything I want to do. She has never told me to close any doors or to steer my path in a different direction. She has wholeheartedly supported every decision I've made, even those she didn't agree with, because she has complete faith in my conviction and commitment. She's believed in me, knowing in her heart that I can succeed and flourish at whichever path I choose in life. And I know she believes in me now.

I understand exactly why she just said what she did. She wants to protect me from the unknown, from the unpredictability of recovery from a broken neck and a severely damaged spinal cord. Just hours after surgery, she's already focusing on what I *can* do, and thus empowering me. I'm not angry or resentful at her response, and I almost surprise myself with my willingness to accept it.

"At least you still have your brain. That wasn't taken away from you," she continues. "I'm so grateful for that."

I suddenly wonder what this process would be like if my brain had suffered as much as my spine, if my abilities to think and communicate were hindered. I'm flooded with a sense of gratitude, but it only lasts a second before I'm confronted with my miserable dilemma again.

Spinal cord injury. I scan my memory to dig up any information I may have about this condition I've only recently learned I have, but I come up with nothing. I try to think of anyone I know who's been through something I might be able to compare to this. But again, nothing.

My mom is still standing quietly next to my bed, squeezing my hands and looking blankly at the bare wall on the other side of the room. I'm not used to seeing her like this. She's usually so chatty, so willing to talk to anyone about anything and everything, but she's strangely stoic now. It's obvious that she's still very much in shock and barely holding it together.

She sighs again, leans down, and gives me a soft kiss on the cheek, as more tears start to well up in eyes. "Arash, you've always done great things in your life, and this injury will not stop you from continuing to do great things. Just remember that."

***

The next time I come to, both my parents are in the room, grabbing their belongings and getting ready to leave.

"Arash jaan, we have to go home," my father mutters softly. *Jaan* is a common term of endearment in Farsi, my native language. My father rarely says my name without this accompanying word.

The hospital's official visiting hours end at 9 pm. Unable to move my neck in any way, I force my eyes to glance toward the clock at the edge of my peripheral vision. It's 10:15 pm. For the second night in a row, the nurses and night shift security guards are being lenient with my family, allowing them to break the rules.

"Okay, Pop. I know. I'll be okay." As I speak, I realize again how dry and pasty my mouth is. Now I can barely talk without my tongue feeling as if it's going to stick to the roof of my mouth.

"Your friend left you his iPad. You can watch something if you get bored." My father suggests a few shows, then positions it on my tray table. "We'll be back in the morning. I love you, son."

"Love you, too, Pop. I'll be fine," I say with zero confidence.

Even now, I can't help wanting to protect my parents from my suffering. I've been this way all my life, always shielding any pain or anguish I go through, for fear of causing them too much distress. This comes from being an only child to extremely loving, caring parents. But this time, my attempt to act tough and calm is probably as useless as a paper cocktail umbrella during a downpour.

My parents quietly walk to the door, turning around to glance at me one last time before they enter the brightly lit corridor and head to the elevator.

Now the only thing I can think about is the dryness in my mouth. It's not just your typical stoner's cottonmouth, induced by one too many bong hits. It's excruciatingly dry. Images pop into my head as I contemplate this brutally uncomfortable situation: *A tumbleweed in a sauna. Getting blasted by a hundred hair dryers from three inches away.*

I tell myself I'm overreacting, that it's not as bad as it seems, and I just need to toughen up and deal with it. I take a few deep breaths. I feel like a dragon breathing fire.

A man's voice interrupts my internal struggle. "Arash, I just wanted to come in and say hi."

A nurse I've never seen before kneels next to me. He's tall and fit, with a warm, gentle face; thin glasses; and a buzz cut of light brown hair. He looks like a cross between a young Bill Gates and a fresh-faced Marine home from duty in Afghanistan.

"My name is RJ. I'll be helping you tonight. I read in the report that you just had surgery. I'll let you rest, as I'm sure you must be out of it. Can I get you anything?"

I try to wet my mouth to speak, but my tongue has turned into the offspring of sandpaper and a prickly pear cactus. My gums and lips are crispy and crunchy. A new image comes to mind: *an 800-degree Neapolitan pizza oven, crackling and burning, its glowing red embers ready to blast the next thin crust that slides in.*

"Water... Could I please have some water, RJ?" I can barely get the words out.

"Bad news, buddy," he says confidently but gently. "Because they operated on the front and back of your neck, just next to your throat, we have to take precautions. You're not allowed to swallow anything yet. No food, no liquids. This is standard procedure following this type of surgery. In the morning, the specialist will see you and she'll determine if you're ready to eat or drink anything. I gotta finish up my notes outside, but I'll be available if you need me."

My heart sinks. I haven't eaten since arriving at the ICU, relying on the steady stream flowing through one of the numerous tubes connected to my body. But the lack of food isn't what bothers me. It's barely 10:30 pm, and the thought of waiting until morning to *possibly* drink something horrifies me.

RJ recognizes my exasperation and does his best to comfort me before he exits. "You're not feeling thirsty because of dehydration; it's because of the medications they used for anesthesia during the operation. Those aren't your typical drugs; they're really strong, and the side effects are pretty brutal. But don't worry: you still have an IV, so you're okay."

Leftover ash stuck on the walls of a roaring fireplace. It's bad enough being laid up in bed, barely able to move my arms and hands, paralyzed through the rest of my body, unable to eat or drink. But on top of so much physical discomfort, to attempt to contemplate the devastation of this injury is too much. I start to feel overwhelmed, and a wave of depression hits me and tosses me in ten directions at once. I try to cry but can't. The tears won't come. It seems impossible that any kind of moisture could come out of my body right now. In fact, if I were able to cry, I'd probably try to lick the tears off my own face.

I remind myself of something I've taken pride of my entire life: my self-proclaimed high threshold for physical pain and discomfort. I think of all the times I hurt something and fought through it, all the times I was in a physically compromising position but refused to accept defeat and kept going. I recognize that this current situation is a hundred times worse than anything I've ever experienced, and I ask myself if I have it in me to be a hundred times more resilient than I've ever been.

Unequivocally, the answer is yes.

I decide that I can get through this night. It can't be *that* bad. At least the morphine and host of other drugs make it so I can't feel the excruciating pain I know is pulsing through my entire body. I just have to deal with this desert in my mouth and make it through to the morning. It's ten, eleven hours hopefully until the specialist comes. I can get there, especially if I can sleep through most of the night.

I give myself a pep talk, take a few deep breaths, try to ignore the strips of Velcro that my tongue and lips have turned into, and close my eyes, determined that sleep will alleviate at least some of this anguish.

Grains of sand in the middle of the scorching Sahara.

Within seconds, my eyes dart open and look at the big analog clock: 10:24 pm. Once more, I try to fall asleep, and to convince myself it's going to happen. Slumber will save me.

What feels like an hour goes by, and I'm still awake. *Tired cigarette butts buried in an overfilled ashtray.* I keep my eyes closed for another eternity, doing everything I can to go to sleep. Accepting my unsuccessful attempt for rest and reprieve, I congratulate myself for my efforts, open my eyes and look at the time.

The hands on the clock don't look much different than when I last checked.

There's no way. It's impossible. I was lying there for so long! It must be a mistake. I conclude that another side effect of the medications must be poor vision, and that I'm seeing double or something. I figure RJ is following the ICU's protocol for treating someone in as vulnerable a state as I'm in, and has been assigned to deal with me, and me only, for better or worse, for his entire shift. That would explain why he rushes in just seconds after I push the call button strapped to my hand.

"RJ, what time is it?" I ask excitedly, assuming a couple of hours have passed since he was last in the room. I intend to explain to him that the big analog clock is broken, that a hospital like this shouldn't have dysfunctional equipment that could mislead patients.

He looks at me for a moment, seemingly surprised by my question, but responds kindly. "It's almost 10:30."

"You've got to be kidding me," I mutter. This is going to be much worse than I thought.

"Try to get some rest, Arash," he says reassuringly as he disappears through the door.

"I just did!" I call after him. "It didn't work."

Searing hot asphalt on a mid-summer day. The frustration in me starts to transform into anger and rage. I force myself to take another deep breath and accept that if sleep won't be my escape, then maybe mindless entertainment will do the trick. I turn on the iPad resting on the tray table inches above my chest. My mind is so jumbled I can barely remember how to operate the damn thing. I conjure up an image of Steve Jobs at the annual Apple World conference, always wearing his signature black turtleneck, confidently standing onstage, holding one of his new products and explaining its features with the brilliant simplicity and lucidity that made him famous—features that right now seem nearly impossible for me to master.

I finally open the first episode of the TV show *Weeds*. "It's a random and funny story. I think you'll probably like it," I remember my dad saying earlier. I'm desperate for anything to take my mind off what's going on in my body, so I give it a go.

A few horribly thirsty, painful hours later, RJ quietly ventures in to check on me. "Oh, you're awake," he says. "I wasn't expecting that. Are you doing okay?"

RJ has been nothing but polite and gentle toward me, so I do my best not to sound too whiny. "So... so thirsty. And everything is hurting now. Shooting pain in my neck, whole body feels like I'm on fire. Other than that, I'm fine," I say, concluding with a sarcastic grin.

He checks his notes for a second and then scrambles into action. "Oh jeez, I need to give you more medication. Usually if you're sleeping, I can wait a bit longer to give you another dose. Have you been awake this whole time?"

"Yes," I grumble.

"Okay, I'm sorry, give me a sec." He scurries to the other side of the bed, just beyond my peripheral sight, and I hear him pushing buttons and wiggling tubes. "Okay, I gave you another dose of the postoperative anesthetics and increased your morphine drip. It will take effect in a sec. You should feel better and hopefully a bit sleepier soon."

I've always been curious about morphine and what it feels like. Not because I've had some crazy desire for ingesting opioids—heroin frightens me to no end—but because I've heard of friends who went through painful surgeries say their dabblings with morphine were surprisingly yet strangely enjoyable. If people are getting addicted to related drugs, then there must be something fun about it. Of course, this is my glass-half-full mentality, always trying to find positivity in an otherwise gruesome experience. I remind myself that as dreadful as this situation is, at least I can enjoy the brief reprieve from the suffering thanks to a powerful narcotic.

It doesn't work.

Within minutes, my pain is gone, but my mental state is worse. I find myself battling fog and confusion, trying to wade through the artificial numbness of the drugs to find my true emotional standing. I get a brief sense of why someone might like the high from powerful medications such as these. They beckon me to come away with them, to flirt with fantasy, to abandon the present, to ignore the agony, to escape any consideration of the future, and just float along in a sedated haze.

Perhaps at some other time this could be fun, but right now—when my world has come crashing down upon me, when everything I ever knew about my life has been turned on its head, when my body is literally lying broken on a hospital bed—the only thing I want is to face reality head on. I don't want numbness, I don't want escape. I want to be able to think clearly and *feel*, to begin the process of coping and to plan for how I will move forward. And these stupid medications are taking all that away from me.

A lonesome thorny bush, baking in the sun on the floor of the Grand Canyon.

"RJ, please, water… anything… my throat is killing me. It's seriously all I can think about." I sound like a lifelong smoker whispering through a bout of emphysema.

His compassion is visible, and his sympathy and understanding unmistakable, yet I can see RJ remembering his duties and responding regretfully. "I can't do it, Arash. I'm so sorry. I can only imagine how bad it is. Please try to do anything you can to take your mind off it."

"What time is it, RJ?"

He gulps, looks at the clock, and knowing now how much it means, he carefully tells me, trying to read my reaction: "It's 1:15, buddy. Stay strong."

Devastation, anger, impatience, and hopelessness surge through me. If I can't make it through one night, how will I begin to put the pieces together and recover from this situation?

I battle with the morphine haze again. I can almost hear its voices telling me to let go and play. I try again to sleep, but it's no use. I'm in so dark a hole and so deep a misery that I have no choice but to start weeping. Yet there are no tears because every bit of moisture in my body has been sucked dry, and each breath is painful. Still, I can't stop. I choke and cough and cry and curse everything I've ever done that brought me here. I start to venture down a path so daunting with regret, fear, despair, and sorrow that I frighten myself silly. What I see down that path is unfathomable. I can't bear even pondering what it has in store for me, so I turn the other way and try to snap myself out of it.

A cactus succumbing to a slow death, digging its roots into the parched earth for any sign of lingering moisture.

I go back to the TV show and give it a couple more episodes, but I can hardly comprehend anything that's going on. Something something, bored housewife, something something, stores of marijuana, something something, kids and lawns and suburbs.

The seconds tick away, each feeling like a minute, each minute like an eternity. I can't stop looking at the clock and wanting this night to end. I want the sun to rise and illuminate the room, I want my family back by my side and I... want... *water!*

I'm desperate now. I push the call button again and look at the clock for the hundredth time.

It's barely past 3 am when RJ shuffles in and I conjure up my inner hotshot lawyer, strutting into the courtroom, ready to plead my case. "Look, man, you have to trust me on this one. I'm as tough as they come, and my pain tolerance is through the roof. Believe me, the last thing I want is to be the annoying, high-maintenance patient who can't handle a bit of a challenge, but this is *torture*. I know your protocol, I understand you can't endanger me, or yourself, and I'm aware that this is a side effect of all that weird stuff you guys put me on. But you have to understand: I'm a stubborn bastard. I haven't taken Advil or Tylenol or any real medicine for almost a decade. My body can't handle this crap. I'm either going to go mental from my dry, prickly tongue and lips or chew them open just to stream some blood into my mouth and relieve this. I can't sleep, I can't focus on anything other than my goddamn desert of a mouth. And I'm too messed up to even cry about it anymore. You have to do something, RJ."

The ensuing expression on his face will likely be implanted in my brain for the rest of my life. He looks at me like a parent who is at once exasperated with and sympathetic to his child. He comprehends just how desperate I am, as he stares at me for what seems like three minutes, sighs heavily, and finally gives in. "Okay, Arash. Let me see what I can do."

When he returns, he pulls up a chair next to me and sits down, leaning over me with his face and hands. "This is the best I can do." He pulls out a thumb-tip-size piece of blue sponge on a stick and a cup of water. "I'll dip this into water and brush it along your lips and gums. I really shouldn't be doing this, just so you know."

"Anything, RJ, anything at all. I'll take whatever you got."

The sponge dances onto my parched lips, and I get a momentary sense of relief. New images momentarily replace the old ones. *A downpour in the Mojave Desert. The shooting flow of a fireman's hose drenching flames. Waves crashing on a blistering beach with the cyclical rise of the tides.*

The fourth time he dips the sponge into the carefully guarded cup of water and back toward my lips, I make my move. Imitating the great white sharks I've seen on nature videos, I snap my mouth open and lunge at the sponge. I bite it and suck out the few minuscule drops of water it holds. Like a guilty cat, I lick my lips and flash a devious grin as I treasure the first bits of moisture hitting my throat.

"Arash! That's not cool! We had a deal. You're not supposed to swallow *anything*."

"I'm sorry, man, but I couldn't help it. That thing had only a single drop of water in it though, seriously."

He knows I'm right, and recognizes the sad-sack despair plastered all over my face. Which is probably why he barely chides me when I do it again a few seconds later, then again, and again. Pretty soon we've entered into a silent agreement. RJ accepts that every three or four dips, I will devour his sponge and extract it dry, and I acknowledge that come morning, no man, woman, child, or supervisory medical professional will hear of his misconduct.

"There's nothing left of this, Arash. You destroyed it." He holds up the sponge like a manhandled corpse, shredded and torn apart with my teeth marks.

My thirst isn't even slightly quenched, but I'm grateful for his act of empathy.

"Can you just stay here, RJ? Tell me a story, anything. This night couldn't feel any longer, I'm going crazy just lying here, and this stupid show doesn't make any sense to me."

"Oh yeah? Well, maybe I can make sense of it with you." He sits back in his chair as he waits for me to resume play on the iPad, which takes me ten times longer than it ever should due to having almost no strength or ability in my hands. I have to flip the iPad around with my wrists and tap at it with my knuckles before I finally hit play.

Within a minute of resuming the show, the only thing I can think about is my parched mouth. I swallow, hoping that some residual micro drops of moisture might remain from the heretofore-sacrificed sponge friend (praise be to him), but I get nothing but prickly, dry air and the sensation of fifty cotton balls smacking around in the roof of my mouth.

And so the seconds drift by, reminding me of the end of a day in elementary school. I'd stare up at the big, round clock over my teacher's head and glare at the second hand languidly ticking along, bringing all of us one second closer to freedom. Even that memory seems like fast-forward compared with what I'm going through now. And to make matters worse, I know that the ability to rapidly move time wouldn't bring me closer to any kind of childlike liberation or joy, but would just continue this waking nightmare.

Apart from the unrelenting feeling of thirst and aridness in my mouth, lips, and throat, the rest of my senses are dull. I still can't understand the TV show because it refers to characters I've never heard of, and past events are mentioned too casually to comprehend without any knowledge of previous episodes.

RJ is quiet but undistracted. What feels like a week goes by, and we've only gone through an episode and a half before he gets up to check his paperwork and ensure that he's not forgetting anything for me. When he comes back into the room, he sees me feebly flailing my arms as I beg him for more relief. This must be what drug dealers have to deal with when their junkie customers run out of finances and grovel for another teeny fix. And junkie I am, except that no drug in the world is worth as much to me right now as a cold glass of H_2O.

He examines me again, trying to compromise with the conflicting voices in his head, then finally sighs his way to a decision. "Ice cubes. That's the best I can do. I'll be right back."

The red paper Coca-Cola cup in his hand as he walks back in is a godsend. *Relief, sweet relief,* I think. Suddenly, I get a swagger—as much of a swagger as one can have lying immobile in bed—and feel a little cocky. I congratulate myself for not only once but twice having convinced RJ to break the rules and alleviate my suffering.

But my celebration is quickly squashed. "I'll give you one cube," he says. "You keep it in your mouth, no chewing or breaking it up, and absolutely no swallowing of any kind. You keep the ice cube in your mouth until it melts away completely."

I nod vigorously. "Sure, yeah, yeah, sure, anything you say, RJ." The junkie is back. *Just give me my fix and I'll leave you alone,* I think.

While I wish he would have wheeled in a pig trough with dirty water and told me to dunk my head in and drain the thing clean, the ice cubes will have to suffice. Unlike my previous transgressions with the sponge, this time I can control how slowly or quickly to melt each precious cube in my mouth.

We continue watching the show and I start to tell time with ice cubes. There's no way for me to cheat because RJ patiently feeds me the cubes one by one. But it doesn't matter. The relief is momentous. It may only be a few drops of water, but the psychological boost I get is indescribable. Now I definitely can't pay attention to *Weeds* or anything but the sweet, succulent gliding of an ice cube swishing around my gums, dancing on my tongue, and trickling down my throat.

"You're a good man, RJ."

He laughs and then goes back into ICU nurse mode. "Remember, you don't tell anyone. I'll hide the evidence afterwards," he chuckles with a grin.

Three small cups of ice later, an episode ends and we discuss our confusion about the show. Just as my new best friend starts to rant about how disjointed the show is, I notice a little box on the iPad screen, next to the title and number of the episode. "Season 3," I whisper. "I've been watching Season 3 this entire time? Well, no wonder nothing makes sense! This damn morphine, codeine, benzedrine, whatever the hell-a-drine shit messed me up! I couldn't even tell that I was watching the wrong season? Jesus...."

RJ hears me rant, and as seems to be his skill, brings peace back to the situation. "Oh well, that explains everything. Guess you'll have to watch from the beginning sometime."

I grumble angrily, frustrated again by the cessation of control brought about by these drugs. I reach my hand up to scratch under my chin, itchy from a week of dirty stubble, but RJ immediately stops me.

"Easy there, buddy. That neck collar of yours has to stay right where it is."

"I know, but my face itches so bad! If it's not one thing, I swear it's something else." I try to scratch around my chin, but my fingers are too weak. I wonder if persistent beard itchiness is yet another side effect of the medication. "You know when your stubble is at that pre-beard stage where it doesn't stop itching? And then I got this collar covering up my whole neck. It's driving me nuts!"

"I know exactly what you mean, Arash." His eyes light up. "You want me to give you a shave, right here? I can't open the collar and get your neck, but I can at least give you a bit of relief on the rest of your face. I'll do it if you want me to."

"Deal."

At precisely 5:37 am, the slowest, most painstaking and unique shaving experience of my life commences.

RJ begins to talk. About what, I have no idea, but he talks and talks. And I listen to every word. It's a time I'll never forget: lying in the bed of an ICU room, the halls so quiet that the only audible sound is the beeping of the machines hooked up to my body, and glancing at RJ's upside-down face as he caresses my face and ever so carefully slides the razor—one of those disposables from the hospital supply closet, to which I would never subject myself ordinarily—up and down my face.

The contents of what he is saying are unimportant. He could be reading the corollaries and articles of some esoteric law, listing the full names of every person in his family tree for the last twelve generations, or reciting the alphabet in Swahili. All I know is that I enjoy every bit of it. The shaving experience somehow distracts me from my thirst and forces me to concentrate my wandering, morphine-laden attention on his voice, instead of thinking of all the separate ways in which I feel violent pain and discomfort throughout my body.

The comfort that slowly envelops me sends me back to childhood again, this time to memories of nuzzling up on my father's lap, listening to Persian lullabies and drifting in and out of consciousness.

***

When I open my eyes again, sunlight is seeping through the half-curtained windows. The ICU is buzzing anew. The smell of weak coffee permeates the hallways, battling the artificial scents of the freshly sanitized hospital floors. A new nurse walks in to greet me, and before she can tell me her name, I pounce on her with my question, unable to hide my panic. "Where's RJ??!"

Her reply is emotionless and vaguely sympathetic, almost patronizing. "Ah, I'm sorry, hon. RJ's shift ended twenty minutes ago. He went home."

I'm relieved that the longest, most tedious, painful, and uncomfortable night is finally over, yet I can't help but feel guilty that I wasn't able to thank RJ again before he left for his empathy, companionship, and care. RJ probably has no idea that at this moment in time, he is my hero.

2.

Slow Rolling in an Ambulance

"You're getting out of the ICU tonight, Arash," the nurse tells me, with what I sense is only partially genuine excitement. "They're going to come pick you up at six o'clock, and we have to start getting you ready."

"What happens then?" I mutter, still battling through the painkillers and sedatives I've been on for the past five days.

"Well, you're covered by Kaiser insurance, so they need to get you to one of their facilities so they can continue to take care of you. Now that it's been over two full days since the operation, they think you're strong enough to be transported."

Even though the John Muir Trauma Center has a partnership with my medical insurance provider, every second I stay here is seen as an unnecessary and extra cost for Kaiser. They want to get me out of this ICU, where my surgery ran up a bill of almost $200,000, and each additional day I spend tacks on another $30,000, and into one of their hospitals. Having had no previous experience with hospitals and operating rooms and ICUs, I have a hard time comprehending why the costs are so astronomically high. I've kept up with current events—it is a presidential election year, after all—and I'm aware of how significant the issue of health care has been. I just never thought that the battle over Obamacare or single-payer or privatized medicine would have such

33

consequential and personal meaning to me. Without wanting or asking for it, I've ended up as an unwanted participant, a casualty of a hot-button issue with massive significance. I curse myself for not having paid greater attention to the intricacies and minutiae of the health-care debates in recent years. Therein might lie some answers and clarity to the sea of confusion I'm drifting through now.

Rage swells up inside me. Rage at a medical system that is based on maximizing profit and minimizing cost instead of wholeheartedly catering to patients' needs. Rage at the fact that they want to move someone who has just endured an unimaginable trauma and seven hours of spinal surgery to a different hospital, just to save themselves a few bucks. Rage at the hospital staff who have become numb to the absurdity of the system, who don't even bat an eye as they move through their tasks, seemingly oblivious to the impact of their actions. And rage at myself for getting into this situation in the first place.

The nurse glimpses the mix of dismay and outright fear on my face and quickly does her best to assuage me. "Don't worry. It's an ambulance transport, they'll get you over there safe and sound. With the sirens off, of course." She giggles.

I wonder how I could be strong enough to do anything other than lie motionless in bed. As I attempt to wrap my head around this upcoming move, I'm reminded of the events that led up to that initial ambulance ride—just five days ago, but it feels like an eternity—that catapulted me into this living nightmare.

I received a phone call that Saturday morning from my coworker inviting me to come to his apartment complex, where he and some friends would be spending the day barbequing next to the swimming pool and enjoying the sunny, warm weather. He had invited me a few times before, trying to convince me it was worth the thirty-minute drive from my urban San Francisco apartment to the suburbs where he lived, and I had always politely declined. But on that cool and cloudy Saturday morning, the thought of escaping to a warmer place and spending the afternoon making new friends seemed appealing enough to borrow my roommate's car and drive east.

The day ended up being as enjoyable as expected, and after a fun afternoon, I was getting ready to head back home when my coworker suggested I stay and go out to dinner with everyone. Usually, I pack my Saturday evenings with activities and outings with friends or family, but on that particular night I had nothing planned. So I decided to stay.

After dinner, when we returned to my coworker's apartment, he immediately realized that he had left his key inside. We were locked out. My keys, clothes and belongings were still in the apartment, so I could not yet leave. We stood in the courtyard of the building as he pointed up at his third-story balcony, stacked directly on top of the two balconies below, and said that when he had been locked out, he had considered climbing up to the balcony and entering through the sliding doors, which always remained unlocked.

I volunteered to give it a try. Why not? I had bouldered and scrambled up plenty of rocks and climbed to the top of fruit trees on many occasions. This didn't seem too bad, and I had confidence I would succeed. In the worst-case scenario, I could bail out and safely climb down to the path below. I hopped up onto the first balcony easily, then pulled myself up and over the railing onto the second balcony, and prepared myself for the third and final hoist up to victory. Every detail of the day leading up to this point is still crystal clear in my mind, as is the memory—the last image from the life I had known for my first thirty years on the planet—of my hands gripping the balcony railing above, in between the hanging towels and still damp swimsuits, and of my feet pushing off and dangling for a moment. And then... it all went black.

The rest of that night was a blur of activity and confusion, with the occasional flash of clarity mixed in. Lying flat on my back on the concrete, seeing the stars above, as the faces jumped in and out of my vision, assuring me that help was on the way. The focused paramedics yelling out questions and commands as they scrambled around and strapped me to the gurney. The wailing sirens and the beeping of the machines I was hooked up to in the ambulance. The white walls of the hospital, contrasting starkly with the blood gushing out of me. The claustrophobic MRI machine into which I was thrust. The many glances of the doctors and nurses as they darted in and out of my fuzzy vision...

Now, the nurse leans in to give me one final, enormous dose of morphine to keep me good and numb for the entirety of the ambulance transport. The paramedics arrive in a flurry, tape my forehead to the headrest to ensure extra support for my neck, and skillfully slide my broken body onto the gurney. I almost get dizzy when, for the first time since I arrived in the ICU, my singular view of the ceiling is replaced by the panorama outside my room.

As I'm being wheeled into the hallway and toward the elevator, Tina, one of the more encouraging and supportive nurses, jumps in front of the gurney and grasps my hand tightly. "Keep fighting, Arash. And visualize, visualize, visualize. Never stop visualizing."

She hugs my parents and gives them some final words of advice that cause my mother to burst into tears for what must be the eighty-seventh time in the last five days. I try again to grasp the suffering I've put my parents through, but the morphine still numbs everything.

I manage a couple of breaths of fresh air, an all-too-brief respite from the stagnant hospital ventilation, as I'm loaded into the ambulance. The paramedic gets in and glances down at my face before he straps another band around my forehead and fastens it to the gurney. "We gotta keep your neck extra safe and stable, doctor's orders." He smiles reassuringly. "My name is Jose, just let me know if I can do anything to help you out. You want to get rid of that thing?" he points down to my right hand.

Since I came out of surgery, I haven't let go of the bright red John Muir Trauma Center squeeze ball that the physical therapist gave me, using the tiny bit of remaining strength and dexterity in my hands to hold onto it religiously through every waking hour. Much like a teddy bear or childhood blanket, the red squeeze ball has comforted me, while also allowing me to make a statement of sorts, to convince myself that as long as I can will my feeble, trembling hands to hang on to it, I'll be able to make it through another day.

"No, I kinda like this thing. Thanks," I whisper as I try to fight through my sedated facial muscles to smile back at him.

The driver leans in and tells me that he's going to do his best to maneuver the ambulance smoothly and avoid any bumps so he doesn't aggravate my neck. "I won't drive any faster than fifty on the freeway, so if you hear any angry honks, just ignore them." He closes the door and turns on the engine, and we rumble out of the hospital parking lot.

Jose starts asking questions about how I got hurt and how I ended up here, and I realize that my responses and explanations feel surreal, as if I'm in a dream and the me I'm describing is someone I don't even know. When I tell him about my fall, about my injury and my compromised physical abilities, again it feels as if there's no way I could be describing my own experience, that it has to be someone else I'm talking about.

There's more energy in my voice when I tell him about my life before the accident: about my job at a solar energy startup that I didn't love but had no intentions of leaving, about the absurdity that I was backpacking on the John Muir trail in the Sierras just last week, and I ended up at the *John Muir* Trauma Center.

Jose says he's thinking of getting a motorcycle, but his wife is worried about the danger.

I tell him about my own, much-adored black motorcycle that I call the Batmobile, and about how much I love riding it. But I admit that the danger is legitimate and should absolutely be considered. "A handful of people, including my mom, who visited me in the last few days confessed that when they first heard about my injury, they assumed it was a motorcycle accident," I tell him.

I can almost him hear gulp as he studies my face and looks at the neck collar, at all the straps holding my head in place, at my quasi-lifeless body. I can guess that he's horrified at the hypothetical thought of a spinal cord injury of his own. It's a look I've seen from my own friends and family—the *holy shit I'm glad I'm not you* look. I'm not certain people realize I've already become familiar with this look. It is indistinguishable from anything else I've observed, and no matter how empathetic or sensitive the person may be, seeing that look is a clear reflection of the horror of my current situation and confirms to me just how feeble and broken I must appear.

Jose's eyes remain fixed on me, and a few minutes of silence pass before he shakes his head, snaps back into life, and pats my wrists. "You got dealt a really shitty hand, boss. No doubt about that. I'm sorry this had to happen to you."

"Me, too."

The ambulance slows down and exits the freeway. I can recognize the tall buildings of downtown Oakland through my peripheral vision as I glance out the tiny window. When the doors open, I'm greeted with the cool breeze and foggy skies of the summertime Bay Area weather that is so familiar to me. Jose leads me into the Kaiser building, which seems old and decrepit compared with the squeaky-clean John Muir Trauma Center, and cautiously maneuvers the gurney through the narrower and more crowded hallways of the Acute Care Department and into my new surroundings.

Before he leaves, he thanks me for sharing my story so openly with him. "Stay positive, Arash, I'm praying for you." He signs some documents completing the transport, gives me one more glance and nod, and leaves the room.

After a few minutes, a young, tired-looking woman pushes her computer cart into the room and sits across from me. She introduces herself as the intake nurse and begins asking questions. "So, what happened to you?"

I see that same look of horror plastered clearly across her face, and I understand that this nightmare has not yet reached its conclusion.

3.

Sitting Tall, Flying High Like a Kite, and Choosing to Live

The shapes on the ceiling have become all too familiar as it has been ten straight days that I've been lying flat on my back in one hospital room or another. Aside from the nurses methodically switching the pillows stacked underneath me every two hours to prevent bedsores, ever so slightly changing the angle of my pathetic view, there has been no break from the monotony of staring up at the ceiling, which now includes not only the dull yellow light bulbs, faded paint, and unexplainable splotches, but also the font size of the brand name for the rusty fan. The obstructive neck brace does nothing to help the claustrophobic inertia that swallows up every minute of the day, leaving only the frequent visits from friends and family to provide distractions from this horrific reality.

The child-size carton of milk and small box of cornflakes sit undisturbed on the plastic tray in front of me, exactly where the nurse left them when she delivered breakfast over three hours ago. The nonstop immobility has resulted in my metabolism crawling to a virtual stop. Even though I'm barely eating any food, I feel satiated up to my throat, as if I've gorged myself on too many trips to an all-you-can-eat buffet. The disgusting sensation of constant imbuement is interrupted only by the uncontrolled bowel movements that are a direct result of my damaged spinal cord being unable to regulate the most basic bodily functions. That said, shitting myself randomly, and then sheepishly asking a nurse to clean me up like an infant, is still preferable to the constipation induced by the anesthetics.

The stale room warms with the light of the sun as it slowly starts to poke its head out through the clouds. I close my eyes and scan my body from head to toe, analyzing each body part, assessing its capabilities, trying to understand what feels impaired and what doesn't. Or rather, what feels *more* versus *less* impaired, as everything has been damaged in one way or another. I acknowledge the novelty of navigating a new—and not improved—body, one that I always respected and never took for granted, yet one that now feels completely unfamiliar. I've been going through this scan dozens of times a day, constantly attempting to determine if anything has changed or improved, comparing what I've been told by the doctors about my body's capabilities to what I actually feel.

I keep hearing the word "quadriplegic" being thrown around in reference to my condition and I don't like it. It makes me feel labeled and categorized, something I've always been careful to avoid. From what I know, the word means I have severe or complete paralysis in all four of my limbs, but when I scan my body, I find this to be untrue. While I undoubtedly feel disconnected to my legs, as if they're now just appendages not serving much purpose, my connection to my upper body is strong. Although I was initially told I should expect little to no movement in my shoulders and arms, I have experienced the contrary. Everyday it seems as if I've gained a little more control as I have made every attempt to fight through inertia and raise and swing my arms around.

My hands have certainly not fared as well and are a far cry from what they were previously. Having played music since the age of four—the violin and clarinet as a child and the guitar beginning in my teenage years—I have always had great dexterity and strength in my fingers, but that is not the case now. I have trouble moving my fingers independently or grasping anything other than that red squeeze ball, which seems to fit into my loose grip perfectly. Nevertheless, I've been conjuring up my strength to try to tighten my grip on the ball, to unstuck my stuck fingers, to wiggle and squeeze and open and close my hands as much as possible, and it does feel that they have been improving, even if it's just the tiniest bit.

Ever since the doctors mentioned yesterday that I was cleared to work with the physical therapists and that I should expect them this morning, I've been waiting eagerly for them to arrive. I have no idea if my body is capable of moving in any way now, but I am hoping they can find some way to get the blood moving, to break this stagnation, and maybe even to give me respite from this view of the ceiling.

So when the two of them walk in the door, I bounce out of bed to meet them—which in my physical state, means I dart my eyes around excitedly and acknowledge their presence loudly: "Tell me you're the PTs? Is it finally time to get moving?!"

"Ha-ha, yeah, that's us. Nice to meet you, Arash, I'm Jenn," says an energetic thirty-something, whose high voice and bubbly personality complement her strong, confident stature. "We're going to see if you're strong enough for us to maybe get you off your back a bit and sit you up. That's probably my goal today. This is my assistant Tom, and he's going to provide most of the manpower to help get you up."

My initial reaction to this rather unambitious plan is immediate frustration. After days of static lying on my back, sitting up can't be the only objective. *Let's hit the gym! Let's get the blood pumping! C'mon, the hard part is over, right? Let's start this recovery!*

Unlike Jenn, who conveys physical competence despite her small size, Tom has a slight, fragile frame reminiscent of a gangly cartoon character, especially with his skinny arms drowning in the baggy sleeves of his light blue scrubs. He can't be older than twenty-five, yet looks like he could easily fit in with a classroom of high school freshmen. He smiles back at me enthusiastically. "Let's do it, Arash!"

After a few diagnostic questions, Jenn leans in and gives me instructions. "Okay, Arash, Tom is going to sneak in behind you to assist you to sit up. Now, what I want you to focus on is your breathing more than anything, and try not to get too dizzy. The biggest challenge right now is your blood pressure getting really low since you've been so static since the surgery. So if you get lightheaded at any point, you have to tell me immediately because it means your blood pressure is dropping and we'll have to lie you back down. And don't strain your neck or make sudden movements with it, okay? We're here to help you with all of that."

"Roger that," I whisper, still not believing this could be so difficult.

Tom looks at me excitedly, his enthusiasm reinforcing his youthful face. He seems up to the task as he sneaks his slender arms underneath my back, jams his bony knees into my hips, and in one move hoists me up to sitting. As I lean back against his legs and he cradles my wobbly torso with his arms, I feel like a puppet with its strings cut off.

I'm immediately shocked by how different the world looks from an upright perspective. I've become so accustomed to looking only straight up at people's faces with the backdrop of the flat ceiling that I've forgotten what it's like to see all the texture and curves and color and details of something as boring as a stale old hospital room. I only have a few seconds to enjoy my new surroundings before I'm hit with the sense of wanting to topple over like a falling tree. The whole room starts to spin.

Tom, who is maintaining an iron grip on my shoulders, starts to show his first signs of struggle. Even though I can't see him behind me, sweat beads are dripping from his face onto my arms, which protrude out of the now-all-too-familiar flowery white hospital gown. His breathing becomes heavy as he continues to hold me up with strained effort.

Jenn stands at the foot of my bed, inches from my dormant legs, staring straight into my eyes, likely attempting to catch any sign of my demise.

As dizzy and awful as I feel, I don't want to give up yet. My competitive nature comes storming out as I decide I'll fake it as long as I have to and do everything in my power to remain sitting up. If it means I pass out, then so be it, but I will not be the fragile heap of bones they may expect me to be.

My eyes must not be conveying confidence because Jenn suddenly bends her knees to be at eye level with me and waves her hands in my face. "Are you okay? Can you see me clearly, Arash? Can you look me in the eyes??"

I mutter something I think is unintelligible, but it provides her enough faith to proceed. One point for my acting! I'm reminded of my night with RJ, of my lawyerly pleas and transgressions, which now feels like it was months ago.

"Just keep your focus on me, okay? If you move your glance around, you may get dizzy," she explains. "Look straight at me, and we'll go from here."

"Oooooohhhhhhkkkkaaaayyyyy…" I mumble, like a dramatic extra slow-motion clip from a movie. I fight against the forces of nature begging me to lie back down and return to the safety of the hospital bed and the tedium of the ceiling panorama.

Tom's entire body is now shaking as he leans up against my increasingly unstable upper back. His grasp of my shoulders is still strong, but the signs of fatigue are apparent in the increasing perspiration sneaking in between his fingers and my skin.

"How are you holding up, Tom?" asks Jenn, undoubtedly noticing that her young colleague may soon be showering me in a steady flow of sweat as this exercise continues.

"I'm… okay, urrggh… I'm okay," he groans.

Jenn's attention shifts back to the swaying guy in the neck collar who resembles a burnt-out hippie performing his intoxicated dance on a music festival lawn. "Okay, Arash, keep your gaze fixed on me and try to sit up as tall as you can. Yes! That's it!"

I'm able to keep looking at Jenn even though everything around her is moving unsteadily. A room with four walls now feels like a hamster wheel, with the windows, the furniture, the countertop stacked with prescription medicine, and the tired curtains taking turns jumping into my line of vision. I suddenly remember the first time I looked through a kaleidoscope as a child and realize I now have my very own real-life version, complete with swirling colors and unimaginable scenes.

I try to breathe deeply, but fail miserably. It feels like there's a heavy vest constricting my chest. I now understand what the pulmonologist meant when he showed up at my bedside just two days earlier and explained that the damage to my spinal cord had dramatically impaired the nerves that control my lungs and breathing. I was only able to inhale one tenth the amount of the air I normally could; but that said, I was still lucky I could maintain my own breathing without the need of a respirator and tracheotomy tube—something almost standard for people with broken cervical vertebrae like mine. He left me with an apparatus I could use to practice exhaling and measure the output of air in my lungs, and instructed me to practice this many times a day. I'm cursing myself now for not practicing these breathing exercises more frequently, as I'm face to face with the struggle to accomplish one of the most basic aspects of human function and something a healthy body does autonomously.

"You're doing great, Arash. Is your blood pressure still okay? Are you feeling dizzy at all?" Jenn asks.

I shake my head, even though it's a lie.

"Okay, now your father is sitting in the corner of the room, a few feet away from me. Whenever you feel ready, I want you to slowly take your gaze off me and look over at him."

I keep breathing shallowly, desperately trying to take a deeper breath and fight off the dizziness engulfing me. I can see my dad in my peripheral vision, sitting serenely but with eyes full of contained excitement, inviting me to shift my glance toward him. I slowly start to turn my head a few inches to the right, battling the swaying walls and moving furniture, and bring my tired gaze over to his smiling face.

"Good job, Arash jaan," he quietly states as he waves at me.

The lightheadedness is overwhelming, but I keep it at bay for what feels like five minutes, but is probably closer to thirty seconds. How could it be that not even two weeks before, I was standing atop a mountain with a fifty-pound backpack, sharing the incredible view of the Ansel Adams wilderness with my friends, and now, even with the help of two people, I can barely sit up in a hospital bed? But contemplating this question is too much for the current moment, as I fight off the near hallucinations I am experiencing as a result of my desperately low blood pressure. It isn't clear how much longer I can keep up this charade.

Thankfully, Tom seems to be of the same sentiment, as the increased sweat from his palms hinders his grip of my shoulders and his breathing gets heavier. I can feel him struggling and squirming, but to his credit, he doesn't raise alarm or let me crumble.

As much as I don't want to admit it, when Jenn finally instructs me to move my gaze back toward her, I'm relieved. I've done my best tough-guy impersonation, I'm moments away from passing out, and I'm exhausted.

"All right, Arash, now before you lie back down, I want you to stay sitting up and to keep looking at me for a few more seconds, okay? I know you can do it. It's important we don't move you up and down too quickly."

I tell myself that the room isn't spinning frantically. "Okay, Jenn, but if the lights go out and I take a dive forward, then I'll blame it on you," I grumble.

After another steady flow of Tom's sweat pours onto me, Jenn finally instructs me to slowly lie down. Gravity is the boss now as I instinctively want to collapse onto the bed. Thankfully, Tom prevents that, as he slowly slides his hands up my back; shifts out from behind me; and cradles my heavy head, still unaccustomed to the bulky neck brace, into the waiting pillows below.

I breathe a sigh of relief and wait for the room to stop spiraling before Jenn leans in to congratulate me. "That's great, you did really, really great!" she says. "I wasn't sure you would be able to do that, but once you were sitting, you seemed confident enough for me to keep going. Take a rest, and tomorrow we can try again and see if we can push it any further."

Tom is practically wringing the sweat out of his shirt as he comes over and says goodbye, with a modest puddle at his feet. They both exit the room, and I hope for his sake that he can shower before he sees another patient.

I can't help but feel baffled by what has just happened. Why did this simple task of sitting up in bed feel so incredibly difficult? What's with all the dizziness? Is it really possible I have physically devolved so quickly that after only a few days of lying on my back in bed, merely sitting up and facing the world from an upright perspective can be such a challenge? The recent memories of standing on the mountain storm back to me and I continue to wonder how I could have regressed so much in so little time…

A nurse enters the room after the PTs have left. "We're late for your dose of pain meds, Arash," she explains worriedly. "I should have given them to you thirty minutes ago, but you were with the PTs and I wanted to let you finish. What's your pain level now, hon?"

I've become accustomed to this question, having answered it every four hours since I got out of surgery. On a scale of one to ten, I have to rate my pain so they can give me the proper dosage of Norco, the opiate painkiller of choice, with massive intoxicating abilities and a host of side effects.

"I guess I'm a five."

"Again? Are you sure you're not in more pain? You said you were a five the last three times we asked!" She looks down at her notes to confirm.

"Yeah, I'm a five."

She stares at me skeptically through her glasses, unable to hide her disbelief. "Even after all that exercise you just did?" She drops her clipboard and walks across the room to clean something up at the sink.

Exercise? What exercise? I think to myself. I was simply sitting up in bed for a few minutes! That's it. How could that be exercise?! The room is still spinning, albeit less kaleidoscopically than before, my vision is still a bit blurred, and the truth is I probably am in more pain than usual, but it isn't always easy to know since my entire body feels numb all the time.

In my early teens, I decided that I would minimize, if not completely eliminate, most pills, especially any painkillers. I told myself that unless it was absolutely necessary (and I recognized the ambiguity in this term), I wouldn't put any medication into my body. And I held true to this vow. So many times, I had seen friends pop a couple of ibuprofen after a long workout or reach for the headache tablets at the first sign of pain. For the most part, I saw these as indications that our society as a whole had become too reliant on pills and tablets and little white bottles to numb pain that, maybe, we were meant to feel. Were we not losing a sense of connectedness to our own physical resilience by constantly taking medication? Wasn't there a long-term benefit to dealing with a few hours of subtle pain?

But then again, I had always been fortunate to have never suffered from significant pain or any major injuries, and I recognized that there were instances, illnesses, or conditions that could easily justify taking medication. Yet, it wasn't these situations that bothered me; after all, I too had happily swallowed large doses of Percocet after having my wisdom teeth removed. It was simply seeing the overreliance on the soft medications, the over-the-counter drugs, and the constant flow of prescriptions that fueled my stubbornness and allowed me to keep my vow for all those years.

As a result, now when they ask me about my pain on a scale of one to ten, my opinion is a bit skewed and I think of ten as the most unfathomable, excruciating, overwhelming pain I can imagine. Surely, only situations such as monks who light themselves on fire in protest or the most barbaric medieval torture of being drawn and quartered could achieve such a lofty measure of agony. That's why, in my opinion, the scale of pain ends at seven, as anything above that seems exaggerated, even though the nurses tell me most patients don't hesitate to say nine or ten on a regular basis. Still, my frequent response of five seems perfectly reasonable, even if it's clearly surprising to others.

Once she has finished cleaning up and pulling the window curtains closed, the nurse returns to the computer stand next to my bed. "Okay, I'm gonna go get your meds. You're absolutely sure you're a five?"

I hold her gaze, assuring her, and myself, of my confidence, and respond, "Yeah, I'm good. Five it is."

She shrugs and comes back to me with the 10 mg dose. I guess she figures I'll find out tomorrow how my system handles everything that's been thrown its way.

***

I've just finished what amounts to my first real bath in the hospital—a cumbersome process involving three nurses, turning me from side to side, and buckets of soapy water and sponges—when I encounter Tom and Jenn for another round of bedside physical therapy. This time is much less eventful as we are all better prepared and the sitting up routine occurs more smoothly than the first time. I don't become quite as dizzy and I'm able to stay sitting up, with the stabilizing effort of an extremely sweaty Tom behind me, for almost ten minutes. I'm even able to perform the very basic, yet very challenging, new arm movements Jenn has instructed for me.

"Are you sure that lifting your arm up isn't hurting your neck?" she asks.

"Not at all," I lie.

In fact, with each inch I raise my arm in front of me, I feel an intense shooting pain in my neck, chest, and back. I try to resist the dominant image that pops into my head: the stitches and staples holding both sides of my neck together playing a game of tug of war with my skin, while trying not to let it rip apart at the tender seams of the scars.

We conclude the session with the agreement that I've improved significantly in just one day's time. It's obvious to me purely based on the lack of those psychedelic visions and swirling colors I witnessed the day prior.

Moments after they congratulate me—and I again hope that Tom has a change of clothes—and leave the room, the pain hits me... *hard*. Suddenly, all the numbness that encapsulated me previously fades away, and there's a searing, severe pain in the back of my neck. My dishonesty with the PTs has come back to bite me. I pushed through the pain, lied about it to them, and convinced myself I could blaze past the paltry limits Jenn or anyone could set for me, but I was wrong.

I lie in bed quietly, knowing my childhood friend Jamie is stopping by to visit within an hour. I try to conjure up all the resistance I have toward medication and prove that I can will myself through this pain, but I have lost the battle.

When the same nurse enters the room and asks me the usual pain question, I respond with sheepish hesitation and embarrassment. "I think I'm an eight."

She stops in her tracks. "Ohh really? You're hurting more today, huh?"

"Yeah... a little... a little more pain," I whimper. By this point, it feels like two daggers have been stabbed in my neck, and with each passing second, they're twisting and ripping into my flesh.

"Okay, here you go, hon. I doubled your dose this time. I'll check on you in an hour, so let me know if you're still in pain."

And so begins my journey with 20 mg of Norco.

Within a few minutes, the daggers in my neck transform into feather dusters gently dancing across my skin. The fiery pain fades away as if it were never there in the first place, and everything seems more cheerful now. My entrance into this blissful high coincides with my favorite time of day, that afternoon hour when the sunlight streams into the room in its orange brilliance. Suddenly, nothing seems so bad anymore. The injury doesn't seem real. The pain isn't plausible, and the hospital just happens to be the most fitting place for me to enjoy this serene intoxication.

Why haven't I done this before? I think to myself. *I've been keeping myself on the brink of physical agony with my 10 mg doses, when I could have been high as a kite this whole time, and loving every second of it.*

My partially open eyelids mask the dancing of my eyeballs, waltzing back and forth into and out of my skull, as my vision intermittently soaks up the illuminated ceiling. My mouth is half open, my lips puckered in a circle like a cigarette smoker deftly blowing rings of vapor into the air. I haven't felt so liberated and relieved since the injury occurred. The same words repeat themselves endlessly in my head: *It's gonna be okay. Everything is gonna be all right.*

I notice that Jamie is standing above me, leaning down from his six foot five frame and gently pressing his massive hand into my upper arm. "Arash! How you doing?" His voice, excited but contained, matches my tranquility.

"Heyyyy, maaaaan… I'm… I'm actually… feeling really, *really* good right now," I say, with my eyes closed and a big smile.

"Wow. That's… um… that's really good. I'm happy to hear that." He's obviously surprised to encounter his friend, who was nearly dead a few days ago, now so calm, grinning like an idiot, and drifting in and out of consciousness.

I have nothing more to say. I am completely stoned. I try to stay conscious for a few more moments to be respectful since he has come to see me, but it's no use. I fade off into euphoria, still feeling the sunlight lulling me to sleep.

***

Beep, beep… beep, beep. It's so quiet now that the machines hooked up to me are more audible than usual. All my visitors are gone. My cousin, who put everything in his life in Washington, D.C. on hold to fly out and spend a few days with me in the hospital, has taken a rare break from my side and gone on a walk with my parents. I hear the nurses outside my room shuffling around, making their rounds, busily tending to the diverse range of needs of their patients. The woman down the hall has started another crying and screaming fit, while two nurses are trying to comfort her. I have heard her a number of times since my arrival in Oakland wailing uncontrollably, for no more than ten minutes at a time, but every few hours like clockwork.

"She hallucinates when her medicines start to wear off," a nurse whispered to me earlier, when we were both overwhelmed by the volume and intensity of her cries. "It takes us some time to calm her down and convince her to take her medication, but once she does, she's okay."

For one of the only moments of the past three days, I am alone. The room is completely dark, matching the nighttime sky and the gloomy, miserable funk I feel immediately as I open my eyes. My opioid-induced afternoon high has worn off, and I'm back to this horrible, awful, devastating reality. I glance around the room and find comfort in nothing. The ceiling, which earlier was basking in the waning daylight, is now still and threatening. My legs are still motionless, seemingly detached from the rest of me, and my hands and arms feel too weak to do anything. I still struggle to hold anything: a fork, a paper cup, a tissue to blow my nose with. My fingers feel like wet cement. My persistent fatigue, intensified by ten days and nights of insomnia, was temporarily relieved by my afternoon Norco snooze. I'm somewhat alert now, which opens the door to a flood of fearful emotions and anxiety.

Previously unable to empathize with the struggles of my family and friends around me because of my constant intoxication and sleeplessness, I now get the first glimpses of what they have been going through, and it's *terrible*. I think of my parents and everything they have experienced for the last week and a half, and the ensuing guilt tears through my entire body and engulfs me. Their worst nightmare has come true, made all the more terrible because I am their only child. All the trust and confidence I have built up with them since my teenage years, when I would leave the house impervious to their concerns, yet always reassure them by safely coming home, has come crashing down upon them since they received that 3 am phone call. I have subjected them to the terror no parent deserves and has no clue how to handle. I imagine them in that moment, jumping out of bed, desperately running out the door, and driving frantically to the ICU to see their unmoving son in critical condition.

A wave of grief slams into me, transforming all the brightness and light from earlier in the day to a heavy, monotonous gray of despair. To make matters worse, the violent pain in my neck is rearing its head again.

News of my accident has traveled quickly to my community of friends, and I've had a steady stream of visitors from the moment it occurred until now. All my friends have been reassuring and encouraging, despite their true thoughts, fears, or expectations after seeing me literally broken and motionless. Never before have I felt so fortunate to have such a caring and considerate group of friends as I do now. I think back to all the people who have come to my bedside the last few days, who have given me handwritten cards, gag gifts, and encouraging messages of support. I glance up at the poster board that one friend dropped off for me earlier, with dozens of messages from my old coworkers and big letters in the middle: "We all love you and are supporting you, Arash!"

Despite the gratitude I feel for the care and support I've experienced, I'm still deep in a depression and sorrow that I've never felt before. I'm somewhat relieved when the evening nurse comes shuffling into my room and saves me from wallowing deeper in my own misery.

"I think you finally got some rest this afternoon, no? Do you feel better, hon?"

I like that the nurses call me "hon," which sounds all the more endearing in their now-familiar Filipino accents. From my frequent conversations with them, I've learned that most of the nurses—the glue holding the hospital together and functioning well—are from the Philippines.

This nurse moves briskly around the room, drawing the curtains and straightening up the chairs my visitors have moved around, then checks my blood pressure and vital signs. "Tell me your pain level, hon, I need to get you your meds."

"Four. Definitely four." I'm actually in quite a bit of pain, the same if not worse than what I felt earlier, but I have no intention of subjecting myself to that emotional roller coaster ride again, even if it means feeling this excruciating pain more acutely. Going back to my 10 mg dose is wise. The medication doesn't completely numb the screaming pain in my neck, but it's enough to leave me in a milder state of discomfort.

Suddenly, I feel a tickle in my throat and start to cough... and cough... and cough. What I feel is simple—nothing more than a bit of phlegm stuck in my chest, swirling around beneath my sternum. For an uninjured person, it would be gone after a couple seconds with a strong cough, but for me, with my dramatically reduced lung capacity and inability to take in more than a couple of sips of air with each inhale, it is the enemy of the state. With every attempt at taking a normal breath, the phlegm intercepts my inhale and throws me deeper into a coughing fit. I don't have enough respiratory strength to clear my chest.

The hours pass, with me coughing and desperately trying to inhale, and with my mom and the overnight nurse sitting by my side, comforting me and making sure I don't choke. My face turns redder as my frustration continues to grow. At one point, the nurse brings an oxygen mask, concerned that my coughing and lack of oxygen are threatening my still dangerously low blood pressure and weak vital signs. More than a few times, I almost pass out.

This has to be a terribly shitty way to die, I think. A thirty-foot fall onto concrete didn't take me out, but a tiny bit of phlegm just might.

Nothing works, not even the oxygen mask, which I'm somehow able to persistently cough right through. It's 4:47 am when a respiratory specialist finally returns my nurse's phone calls to discuss the worst-case scenarios and potential treatments. After a few minutes of discussion, the decision is to give me another hour or so and attempt the oxygen mask again before taking more dramatic action.

It's at this precise moment, when a worried nurse straps a different mask across my face, with a seemingly minor yet life-threatening cough in my chest, with my mother crying endless tears above me, horrified that she can do nothing more to help her only child, that the gravity of my condition and the path I choose to embark upon become crystal clear. I will not succumb to some loose phlegm in my chest. I will not accept a broken neck and let a severely damaged spinal cord rob me of my strength and my will. I will not allow medication or any external factor numb me to my own pain. At least I am *able* to feel the pain. At least that line of communication between my brain and the rest of my body is still open, even if so many other parts are impaired.

So little information has been given to me about my future; about the possibility of any kind of recovery. Every time I bring it up or ask questions to the medical practitioners who have zoomed in and out of this strange nightmare that I've been living, I have been met with blank faces, vague statements, and pleas to be patient, to trust that more answers will come soon. Now, after struggling with each inhale and exhale and fighting to make it through this night, I suddenly know that no matter what I'm told, I will give it my everything. I may not know my boundaries or limits yet or have any clue of how my body and spirit and soul will respond to this nightmare, but I *will* respond. I *will* live. I *will* thrive.

What remains to be seen now is how.

4.

Diagnosis and Prognosis

It's the tenth consecutive morning I have woken up flat on my back and barely able to move, and the hospital is fresh with a new day's supply of frenetic activity. That familiar stale smell of weak coffee and artificial cleaning liquid is wafting through the hallway and into my room. A nurse comes in and tells me that a bed has opened up at the inpatient rehabilitation hospital in Vallejo, and I will be leaving Oakland within twenty-four hours. With this news also comes a sudden and continuous flow of visits from various specialists, who take my blood, test different functions, and generally do their due diligence before I'll be out of their hair for good. Every time I think that the tests are complete and I start to talk to my mother and cousin—who has come for an early visit because he is about to get on a plane to fly home—we are interrupted by a new person coming into the room, jabbing a needle into my arm, drawing more blood, and asking me more questions. I am told that in a few minutes I will have the most important visit of all, from Dr. Lisa Johnson, my physiatrist, or *doctor of rehabilitation*, a term I only recently learned, who is in charge of officially diagnosing my injury.

My mother looks first at my cousin and then at me. "What do you think she's going to say? How will she do a diagnosis?"

My cousin shrugs and looks at me worriedly. "I guess they must use some sort of sophisticated device. That's my guess, anyway," he says.

We have only a few silent moments to contemplate this before a middle-aged woman with a warm smile cautiously enters the room and approaches my bed. "Hello, Arash. I'm Dr. Johnson. I've been meaning to pay you a visit, so it's a good thing I'm able to catch you now, before we ship you off later today," she says as she reveals a unique and endearing loud chuckle. "We should talk a bit about your injury and some specifics because I'm sure you have lots of questions."

"Yes, I do. And I'd love some answers."

"Well, I'll do my best!" She chuckles again, more loudly this time. "I'm going to tell you a bit about myself so you understand my background, as I can relate to at least some of what you're experiencing."

My eyes widen as she describes her career path and explains how she ended up in this profession. She speaks in carefully crafted sentences that are refreshingly free from esoteric doctor-speak, with her chuckle filling in like punctuation marks: "I suffered a traumatic brain injury at age seven that impaired my physical and mental development and prompted the doctors to tell my family that the damage would likely be irreversible." She goes on to share many details of her childhood and the impact of her brain injury: how she became incentivized by her desire to prove the doctors wrong, and how that ultimately allowed her to recover from her injury, attend medical school, and specialize in rehabilitation medicine. She clearly provides a unique perspective to this complex field of study. I appreciate her authenticity and candor and that she is the first medical practitioner I've met who has chosen to share about herself and go beyond standing over me and talking dryly about what *has* happened and telling me what *will* happen, like some clairvoyant decree.

"Now, let's talk about you," she concludes. "Did you know anything about spinal cord injuries before this happened?"

"Not a thing. I still don't know much. I guess I've been waiting for this conversation before I went too deep down the rabbit hole of website explanations and Wikipedia."

"Good. Let me give you the basics." She reaches for a model of a skeleton on wheels that she has brought in, but the spine and body separate from the head and tumble to the ground. "This dang thing, always giving me trouble!" She chuckles again as she puts the model back together. I can't help but recognize the irony of this mishap as I watch her screw the spine back into the model's skull.

Dr. Johnson starts to describe the structure of the spinal cord, of each nerve that branches out of every vertebra, and how each controls certain specific sensory and motor functions throughout the body. I'm impressed at the complexity and ability of the spinal cord as I learn that practically every function of the body, conscious or autonomic, is controlled by this bundle of communication that runs down our backs. As she transitions to speaking specifically about my injury, I'm able to make sense of the impairments I've been experiencing in this newly unfamiliar body: contracting any muscles below my chest, breathing deeply, body temperature regulation, bladder and bowel control—all have been affected by the tremendous shock to my spinal cord.

Strangely, as I absorb all this information, I feel completely removed from it, as if it has nothing to do with me. I still haven't come to terms with the reality of my injury or that it has happened to *me*. Much like the initial conversation I had with the neurosurgeon following my operation, everything still feels surreal, as if at some point the director will yell "cut!", the scene will end, and everything will all go back to normal. Almost immediately, I'm snapped back into reality.

"Typically, a C5-C6 SCI like yours will result in damage to the nerves that control shoulder, tricep, wrist, hand, and finger function," she explains. "The fact that you have some volitional movement in your hands is good because that's not what usually happens. Also, because you have some sensation throughout your body, your injury is likely incomplete, meaning that your spinal cord is not completely severed. That's a good thing."

I have a hard time comprehending how anything about my situation could be good, but I bite my tongue and let her continue.

"SCIs are assessed using a system created by the American Spinal Injury Association (ASIA), with levels A, B, C, and D. Unlike grades in school, and to no understanding of mine, the order is backwards: A is the worst as it implies a complete injury, a total sever of the cord, with no sensation or motor movement below that level in the spine. With an ASIA A injury, there's less than a one percent chance of regaining significant function."

While a one percent chance is a terrible probability, it's strangely comforting to me. I suppose that because I expected the news to be worse and that any talk of odds or percentages of recovery would be limited to zero, as soon as I find out there is a chance, no matter how tiny it may be, I know there is hope.

My method for dealing with a challenging situation in life has always been to accept and prepare for the worst so as to avoid anything unexpected, and if things turn out better, then it's a pleasant surprise. *One percent?* I think to myself. *Well that's not so bad, that means I have to be that one guy out of a hundred who's more motivated than the others. I can be that guy*. This is also my way of protecting myself from her forthcoming prognosis. If the worst case is a less-than-one percent chance, then I have to start there, and expect that this will be me.

She goes through the different ASIA levels of injury, confidently stating various percentages and categorizing each type of person by the extent of his or her disabilities. "ASIA B injuries will likely be able to do *these* things and live *this* type of life; ASIA C injuries will be able to do a bit more but be limited in the following ways," and so on.

It all sounds too confident, as if the numbers and percentages could predict actual potential and dictate success. Until now, I've liked Dr. Johnson, her demeanor, and her patient approach and attention to detail, but hearing about the predictabilities of the different types of injuries raises a huge red flag for me. I feel doubt building within me. I understand that patients want answers from their doctors and want to know what to do and not to do, and that therefore doctors share the information they have, as well as percentages and categories of success or failure, or of living and dying. I think of all those times in movies and TV shows when the doctor comes to the patient's bedside and with subtle but dramatic music in the background, tells the patient, "You have an X percent chance of survival." Now, she's that doctor, and I'm that patient. I'm the one being told those numbers, and although they don't make sense to me, I'm somehow supposed to believe them, to accept this narrative, to play out this real-life movie.

"Okay, Arash, it's time for me to do the ASIA test and come up with a diagnosis of your condition." With that, Dr. Johnson pulls out an extraordinarily high-tech piece of equipment that will be used to make this massively important assessment and to frame my emotional state for the days, weeks, and possibly years to come. It's a safety pin.

To say I'm confused is a massive understatement. I was expecting a fancy technological marvel that would somehow scan my brain and spine and come up with all kinds of zigzagging graphs and sophisticated analytical models. But this? A safety pin?!

"I want you to close your eyes, and as I poke the different parts of your body with one side of the pin, say immediately if it's sharp or dull. Please don't guess, and don't cheat by looking at where I'm poking you. If you don't respond right away, I'm going to assume there's some impairment there. Are you ready to start?"

I still can't get over the fact that my official prognosis is coming down to the imperfect science of getting poked by a safety pin and yelling out my response like I'm flipping a coin, heads or tails. In fact, I could guess every single time and have a fifty percent chance of being right. What would that mean? How accurate or predictive can this method be?! I glance over at my mom and cousin, who are standing just behind Dr. Johnson. They lock eyes with me, seemingly trying to communicate their own healthy skepticism, and give me a nod of tentative reassurance.

"All right, let's get it over with," I mutter.

The assessment lasts ten minutes and consists of exactly what Dr. Johnson described. She pokes me everywhere, covering every limb, moving methodically up and down each side of my body and giving me little time to process the pokes before moving on to a new location. Except for some patches on my biceps and forearms, everything above my nipples feels close to normal. My stomach, hips, and upper thighs are where things get very muddy. I can tell exactly where she is poking me, but the sensation is not keen enough to distinguish between sharp and dull. To my surprise, though, as she moves down to my ankles, feet, and toes, the sensation gets clearer again. I am able to feel the annoying little prick of the pin bouncing on my skin, especially on my left foot.

There is one final part of the assessment after the safety pin adventure is over, and as soon as I see her putting on a latex glove, I know what's coming. She hesitates, and then speaks as the glove snaps tight around her wrist. Again, it seems like I'm living out a scene from a movie. "I know this will be uncomfortable," she says, "but I have to test the sensation in your rectum to see if any of those lower nerve connections are intact."

"Do what you gotta do, doc," I say, not hiding my exasperation. I feel guilty for every dumb joke I've ever made with friends regarding this exact situation, and cringe at the fact that I am now the butt of all those jokes... pun intended.

As soon as she inserts her finger I yelp, surprised by my inability to control the volume of my squeals.

"Oh, that's really good, Arash!" She quickly throws away the glove and starts washing her hands. "The fact that you have rectal sensation, along with your patchy sensation throughout your body, shows that your injury is incomplete." She scribbles down some notes and carefully examines her folder, before she finally ends my anticipation. "Incomplete C7, ASIA B. That's the official diagnosis of your level of injury. That means that above your C7 vertebra, your functions are relatively normal. It's below that the neural connections are damaged."

At this moment, for the first time since I entered the hospital, I burst into an uncontrollable bout of tears. I bawl and wail and weep and whimper. My mother follows my cue and instantly explodes into tears of her own. She leans in and hugs me close, implying somehow that this embrace will allow us to persevere through our intense despair.

Knowing the prognosis does not comfort me or give me great optimism. My crying has nothing to do with what Dr. Johnson said. It's just the fact that *something* has finally been said and formalized about my body and my injury that allows the emotions I've contained within me—as I lie here, numbed with painkillers and bandaged with the love of my family and friends—to explode out.

Dr. Johnson patiently waits until my crying has subsided and then gives her final comments. "Usually with your type of injury, it's almost impossible to regain the ability to walk again. Whatever recovery is going to happen will probably happen in the first year or two. Anything beyond that is highly unlikely. The truth is that it will take time. A year... two... maybe more, but you have to be patient. The good thing is you're going to the right place now. At the inpatient rehab hospital in Vallejo, you'll receive the necessary therapy you need to get better. Just get ready to work hard and try to stay positive."

My first reactions are questions. I don't voice them aloud, but they rattle around in my mind: Why is her language, and the language of the other practitioners who've talked in more general terms about my future, always framed so passively? Why are my improvements referred to as something "that will happen," as if they're out of my control and independent of my efforts and commitment? Is it not logical to assume that an individual can influence his or her future? This entire paradigm through which the medical establishment has treated me and my injury, and how it now predicts my recovery, feels completely flawed. Although the tears on my face are still fresh and my confusion about everything in my life feels overwhelming, a strange sense of calm and clarity envelops me.

Three words repeat in my head. *I don't care.*

I don't care what they say. I don't care what the percentages are. I don't care what the stupid safety pin was supposed to predict. I don't care if they think I am the most stubborn bastard in the world who insists he will take matters in his own hands. I don't care what they tell me about my body because *I'm* the only one who can feel my body from the inside, who knows that I'm not detached from my lower body, that I'm not dead or dormant from my chest down. I don't care if they think this injury is some kind of sentence I have to accept and adapt to.

I will be that one percent, or one tenth of one percent, or one hundredth of one percent, or whatever percent that will improve beyond what they have projected for me. I will remain in conversation with my body for every moment going forth. I will listen to what my legs and feet and stomach and hands are telling me. If I can feel the slightest touch on my foot and on my toes, then who's to say I can't use that sensation to help me regain movement there? Who's to tell me I should abandon hope or faith in recovery? And who's to tell me my body has some strict countdown timer, and that the healing will suddenly conclude after one or two years?

Dr. Johnson's diagnosis and prognosis do little to help me understand what will happen in the future, but they clarify within me a deep sense of resolve and motivation. If I'm to maximize my recovery, I will have to do it my own way. I will have to rely on myself, and on the love and support of my family and friends and community, to set out and achieve what I think is possible. I now realize I must make preparations for what is to be a long and arduous fight. I may be lying motionless on a hospital bed, but the fire inside me has been ignited, and four barrels of gasoline have been dumped on top. I make a commitment to myself, right then and there, not to let this fire burn out.

I thank Dr. Johnson as she excuses herself and makes her way toward the door.

Before she exits, she stops and says one last thing: "This is likely the worst it will be, Arash. Hopefully, things only get better from here."

I crack a smile and nod.

As my mom wastes no time and starts to pack up my belongings, I mentally prepare myself for what is to come in the morning: another farewell from the nurses and hospital staff, another gurney I will be strapped onto, another ambulance ride, and a journey to Vallejo to begin the next chapter of this saga.

5.

Expectations, Ambitions, and Goals

"What are your goals for physical therapy here with us, Arash?" Rick is looking at me intensely with energetic green eyes that convey intense concern at the same time as a boyish wonder.

It is the first day in my third hospital of the week, and I'm slowly starting to learn my surroundings. There are a variety of different people in the acute neurological inpatient rehabilitation unit of Kaiser Hospital in Vallejo, a blue-collar, downtrodden aesthetically unimpressive city. It's the home of a large air force base, as well as a famous rapper from the early 1990s, and is one of the most ethnically diverse urban populations in the nation. Its recent history includes municipal financial struggles and near bankruptcy. Its location, only thirty minutes east of the well-heeled hipster cafes and trendy restaurants of San Francisco, yet worlds apart culturally, passes like a blur as you drive the well-trafficked corridor between the Bay Area, Sacramento, and Lake Tahoe. I've driven through Vallejo dozens of times, always without giving it a second thought, forever on the way to somewhere epically more interesting. Now, however, I find myself a resident of its shiny new hospital, tucked into a quiet residential neighborhood.

When Kaiser Permanente, one of the largest medical insurance providers in the country, recently renovated this hospital, one of their objectives was to build a world-class rehabilitation unit for people who had suffered spinal cord injuries, a stroke, traumatic brain injuries, or other neurological impairments. Any Kaiser member in Northern California with a severe neurological condition vies for one of the few available spots in this well-regarded rehab unit. The physical therapists are known to be among the best in the region.

Dr. Johnson's assertions about this place are confirmed as the air of everything here is more "let's get active and moving" and less "lie in bed all day, with the nurses doing everything for you." This wing of the hospital was built a year or two ago, so it still has that extra squeaky clean, shiny, sparkly vibe, which is a stark contrast to what I saw in the last hospital: the inexplicable stains on the walls, the outdated furniture, the inefficient building design, and the waiting rooms that had endured too much waiting in them.

I was told before I met Rick that he was going to be the main physical therapist in charge of my rehab, that I would be working with him nearly every day. So now as I meet him for the first time, I'm eager to make our interaction a positive one. That said, his first question, about my goals for therapy, baffles me. I have no idea how he could be so clueless as to not know the one and only goal that has consumed me and framed my recovery.

"I want to walk," I say, with only a slight sense of annoyance.

At the beginning of our conversation, Rick talked about the hospital; he familiarized me with the different gyms and hallways and showed me the equipment I would be using. He seemed like a smart, motivated therapist who is genuinely passionate about his work and very skilled. In fact, he's a year younger than me, and his avid love of running, biking, and the outdoors, along with his commitment to Bay Area sports teams, means we have a lot in common. I already get the sense he sees some of himself in me—he turned red and gulped loudly when I told him my age and background. He's probably considering how my physical injuries would feel within his own body. The older and more experienced PTs who trained Rick told me how bright he is and how much he has learned about neurological rehabilitation, which explains why he has risen through the ranks at such a young age. Needless to say, I feel like I'm in good hands. But while I generally get a positive vibe from him on this first day, I can only wonder again why he is asking me such a ridiculous question.

I repeat myself, not knowing if he heard me the first time: "I want to walk."

He looks at me with a puzzled stare, probably wondering if I've seen myself in the mirror at any point in the last few days or have any idea how damaged I am. He sighs and continues to stare blankly, apparently not knowing what to say. Nine minutes into our meeting, and I've already stumped the poor bastard.

"Look," I continue, acknowledging his apprehension, "I realize I'm in bad shape right now, and maybe it's not that realistic that I walk out of here tomorrow, but the only goal I have—the only thing I can conceive of—is to walk. So show me how to do anything that will put me on that path."

"Um... Okay..." He sighs incredulously, trying to hide his exasperation, while he maintains his quizzical stare and searches for the proper words. "You see... usually... um, we have to pick some... some short-term, more realistic goals to work toward, so we can justify the therapy we're doing with you. With your level of injury, walking just isn't a realistic or functional goal now. So maybe we can start with some smaller goals, more everyday things you might want to work on?"

I feel like a broken record. "I don't know what can be more everyday than walking, but that's the only thing I can think about right now. I'm not sure what other everyday things you could be referring to."

Rick finally sees an opening. He shrugs off my bluntness and continues patiently: "Why don't we start with functional goals, like... like transferring from your bed to your wheelchair or sitting up safely without any back support. That will help you with other kinds of transfers. Then maybe we can move on to you transferring from your wheelchair to a shower chair or commode."

The words *"your* wheelchair" make my skin crawl. There is an implied permanence in the way he says it's my wheelchair that almost prompts me to end the conversation right then and there, and wheel my pathetic ass back out into the hallway. It hasn't even been two weeks since all of this happened, and for him to expect me to know the movement challenges that come with using a wheelchair is unreasonable.

On top of that, my insurance company has notified me that when I'm discharged from the hospital in a few weeks, I will have to pay for my own wheelchair; it's not covered under my plan. It enrages me to think that the hospital and my insurance have already decided when they want to discharge me from their care, yet have refused to pay for the most essential piece of medical equipment needed at that time. How am I supposed to exit the hospital doors if they don't provide me with the means to do so? I want to yell at Rick and tell him that for now, it's not *my* wheelchair, but *his,* and I still don't know what he expects from me regarding shower chairs or commodes.

"Rick, I've never heard of a commode, so how am I supposed to know I will need to transfer onto it? And if I can walk, then I probably won't even need a commode, right? So I'm sticking with my original goal. I want to walk."

He ignores my rebellious remarks and responds calmly. "A commode is just a seat that sits above the toilet, for when you need to do your bowel program."

My bowel program?! I think. Why is every bodily function being turned into an event of some kind? Why not refer to it as what it's always been and always will be: pooping, shitting, defecating, number two, taking a dump, etc. All of a sudden I have to start referring to one of the most basic human activities as "my bowel program"? My blood is starting to boil, but I try to hold it together. "Fine. I suppose that all makes sense. But all of it is new to me! I don't know anything about these transfers or movements or anything involving *this* wheelchair, so how would I know to set goals like that? I feel like you're asking me to know things about a body I'm unfamiliar with and still trying to figure out."

Rick's face tenses as he possibly recognizes that his question needed more clarification or perspective. Because he strikes me as someone who has genuinely good intentions and cares about his work, I decide to ease up a bit. I swallow and bury the tears that are welling up in my eyes and do my best to match his good nature. "Look, man, I just want to get better. I'll do whatever is necessary to get stronger and get out of this wheelchair. But can we get moving, already? I'm so damn tired of sitting and lying still."

Rick cracks a smile, sighs reassuringly at my change in tone, and tosses his clipboard down as he jumps into action. "Okay then, let's get to work."

6.

Nancy

"Seven... eight... nine... ten... And take a break. Nice work, Arash." Rick grabs the weighted rubber ball out of my hands and leans me back against him so I can rest.

I'm finally able to release my arms down by my sides, as I sit back on the therapy table and glance around the room at all the activity going on with the other PTs and patients. It's the middle of my second full week in rehab, and things have changed considerably from the days of lying immobile on my back. My schedule now consists of two hours of physical therapy and one hour of occupational therapy every day. The only exception is Sunday, when everything shuts down, the gym doors all remain locked. Last Sunday, I had to fight through the tedium and monotony of inactivity by wheeling up and down the empty hallways with visiting friends and family.

Just as I'm readying myself to continue my exercises, a woman darts her motorized wheelchair right in front of me and smiles excitedly.

"Hi, I'm Nancy!" She has long, straight, silver hair messily held back by a purple hair tie; a thin face with the first semblance of wrinkles illustrating her sixty-plus years; and a long-sleeved black blouse that hugs her thin arms and bony collarbone. "You're Arash. I've been meaning to find you for the last couple days and introduce myself. Good to see you working hard. How are you feeling with everything?"

It's a question that may sound simple but has a massively complicated answer, and I do my best to respond courteously without being too dismissive. "Hanging in there, I guess. Just doing my best," I mutter, already thinking about the corrections I'm going to make to the next round of core stability exercises with Rick.

"Yeah. That's good. That's really good. Just don't get too frustrated right now, it will all get easier."

That's a pretty presumptuous thing to say to someone you met seventeen seconds ago, I think.

"I had my accident forty years ago, and back then we didn't have any opportunities like this," she continues, with more than a little resentment. "But I think I've made it through life pretty well. I got married and started a family, raised a wonderful daughter, and made the most of my situation. You know, there's so much more to life than this injury; it's important to remember that."

I'm utterly perplexed at how, in the matter of two or three sentences, she has progressed from a simple introduction to providing intimate details about her family life, along with unsolicited life lessons. I expect her to recognize that I'm losing valuable moments of my precious hours of PT, and to graciously end the conversation she initiated. But she just stares at me, expecting a response.

"Right. That's a good point. Thanks for sharing that," I say, giving her the benefit of the doubt and assuming she has the social awareness to accept my curt replies as evidence of my disinterest in chatting in the middle of my workout.

But she continues talking. She explains that she's an employee of the hospital who is here to answer patients' questions, provide moral support, and educate people about the many details of life with a spinal cord injury. She says she will be teaching next week's informational session, which I am required to attend as part of my therapy.

After a few more minutes of her talking and nothing more than polite nods from me, Rick jumps in and tells her we have to get back to work.

Her obliviousness finally fades, and she bids us farewell—but not before she has given herself another plug: "The information I'm going to discuss next week is really useful, and I'm looking forward to sharing it with you, but I'll see you before then. I like to pop in and say hello to people. I'll be giving you lots of opportunities to speak with me. See you later!"

I don't give much thought to the strange conversation that just occurred, as I'm relieved to get back to my therapy.

***

The next day, another awkward interaction with Nancy ensues.

This time it's during my occupational therapy session, just after I've finished submerging my hands in buckets of ice water to shock my nerves and relax my finger muscles so I can strengthen them. I'm wincing and breathing heavily, fighting the intense nerve pain from my forearms as a result of being in the freezing water for more than a minute. Despite the pain and throbbing discomfort, I've come to appreciate the effects of the ice dunking because it allows me to have more dexterity in my semi-paralyzed fingers and hands, especially in the twenty to thirty minutes immediately following the ice.

I'm staring at a wooden tray full of screws of various sizes and contemplating how I will perform the task of pinching my thumb and index finger together to pick up each screw, extend my arm forward, and place the screw into a small jar. While I'm fortunate to have retained some minimal movement in my fingers, this exercise is particularly challenging and requires significant focus. As I reach for the first screw, fighting the paralysis and trying to will my hand to obey me, Nancy rolls up next to me.

Unapologetic about breaking my concentration, she launches straight into conversation. "Hey! I told you I'd see you again! Looks like you're doing more good stuff here." She glances at the wooden tray—which doesn't appear to be of any interest to her—then back at me. "So what's new with you today?"

I'm immediately reminded of our less-than-inspiring interaction from the previous day, yet can't help but conjure all the lessons on civility and courtesy I learned from my parents. Rudeness has no place in conversations. Regardless of someone else's manners and how that person talks to me, it's my responsibility to maintain respect and graciousness. I disregard my instinct to blow Nancy off and decide to give her another chance, and open up to her just a tiny bit. "I'm doing all right, Nancy. It's so frustrating not to be able to use my hands the way I used to, but everyone keeps telling me I'm lucky to have the limited function I have right now. So I'm trying to make the most of it and get them stronger."

"Oh... I see..." she starts, looking down at my hands. The fleeting expression on her face seems to be of slight resentment as she jumps into a diatribe about her own hands. I notice for the first time that they are still quite impaired. She speaks in a scattered monologue, without pauses, haphazardly bouncing around between details about her own injury and more unsolicited suggestions for my everyday life. After a few minutes, I give her a not-so-subtle hint by turning so my immobile neck is facing away from her, and going back to my task with the screws. But it doesn't work.

She keeps talking, demanding my attention, unaware that my fragile patience has run dry. She finishes her ramble and waits for me to respond, but my politeness is now a thing of the past. We both sit in silence as I stare down at the screw that is wedged between my finger and thumb, and just about to slip out of my almost-nonexistent grasp.

She brings her attention back to the tray and watches me struggle with the screw, which falls to its inevitable demise. "Well, even if your hands don't get any stronger than they are now, at least you'll have no problems working the joystick on a power chair like mine!"

I glare at her shamelessly, and see that same look of resentment flash across her face. I wonder if she realizes that her last statement has upset me more than I can comprehend. *No improvement in my hands? A power chair like yours? What's with those assumptions, lady? Where's the encouragement and positivity I so desperately seek?*

"Have a good day, Arash." She badly mispronounces my name as she heads out the door.

"Bye, Nancy," I call after her.

That night, my mother tells me about her own encounter with Nancy, which also sounds awkward, if only a bit less than mine. "She told me about her own injury and how she got through it. Oh, and she talked a lot about raising her daughter, and what it meant to be a mother despite her injury. She seems like an... *interesting*... person."

I chuckle to myself because I know my mother too well not to recognize that "interesting" is filling in for another word she can't identify or is too polite to use. Knowing that my mom is a great judge of character, I assume she has some of the same apprehensions about Nancy I have, but I decide not to do any more than nod in acknowledgment.

"Well, the hospital has her on staff for a reason. Maybe she has some good perspectives and stories to share," she concludes.

Nancy becomes my very own Cheshire cat from *Alice in Wonderland*, popping up unexpectedly and repeatedly nearly everywhere I go. I begin to wonder if she's received some kind of directive from the higher-ups to always track people down while they're in the middle of their therapy sessions; I notice that she has a habit of inserting herself into patients' PT and OT sessions, before moving on to the next person. I try to justify her actions by telling myself that the neurological rehab unit of the hospital isn't a large area, and aside from patients' private rooms, which I assume to be off limits, the spacious and humming PT gym and the smaller yet still buzzing OT room are two of the only places where people will reliably be throughout the day.

All I have heard since I woke up in the ICU is how debilitating this injury is, and how difficult of a struggle it would be to regain any significant function, should I choose not to—figuratively speaking—throw up my arms and surrender. That, according to most of the medical staff, is the most common option. When I found out that Kaiser Vallejo was supposed to be such a fantastic place for rehab, with access to some of the most experienced staff in the area, I expected my two hours of physical therapy daily to be the jumping off point for my long, incredibly arduous road to recovery. As a result, I'm always on time for my sessions and always want them to last longer than the allotted time. I make it my objective to squeeze all I can out of literally every second of PT. I don't act this way because I want to be an annoying, prickly patient, but only because I assume everyone else is doing the same thing.

I mean, wouldn't all those in this hospital unit, having gone through a severe neurological injury, show up to their therapy sessions chomping at the bit, ready and willing to do anything to improve their situation, no matter how impaired they may presently be?

That should be a rhetorical question, but apparently it's not. In fact, I find that I have a newfound anxiety. I am constantly looking over my shoulder in expectation that Nancy will show up out of nowhere and eat up valuable minutes of my therapy. This is how it goes for the next few days. I am doing my best to dodge this seemingly well-meaning yet socially inept woman whom the hospital has hired to do precisely what I want to avoid; namely, talk to me about adapting to my current physical state. I'm not completely opposed to talking to her, I try to convince myself, I just don't want it to be in the middle of some activity.

***

As I'm struggling to hold the wired remote with my floppy right hand as I use my left thumb knuckle to push the button and raise the back of my bed to sitting, I notice a new item on the breakfast tray in front of me. When I am sitting up, I examine it more closely. The small yellow carton with "Health Shake" printed in large letters looks like something out of a 1960s TV commercial. I get the black-and-white image of well-kempt nine-year-old boys with tidy combovers in a school cafeteria, smiling as they sip the beverage and proceed to run out to their mitts and baseball bats on the playground.

I take a small sip through the straw stuck in the carton. The taste of chemically chocolate milk with a hint of chalk coats my mouth before I can spit it out. *What kind of "health" is in this thing?* I wonder. I read the ingredients and find a long paragraph of unfamiliar and unpronounceable items: sodium hexametaphosphate, ferric orthophosphate, alpha tocopheryl acetate, and more. These are the ingredients for health?

Each day, I'm given the opportunity to order anything I want from the hospital's menu. The items I've sampled so far range from a smelly hamburger to dry, doughy pancakes to oatmeal as stiff as cement mix. Because I want to remain as healthy as possible, I've opted for a small box of cornflakes every morning, supplemented with fruits and smoothies my family and friends have generously trafficked into the hospital for me. So I'm not certain how this so-called health shake ended up on my breakfast tray, and I find myself more than a little upset as I extrapolate how this reflects on the health-care industry's definition of a healthy diet.

Since I'm here to get better, shouldn't I be avoiding a bunch of chemicals and synthetic additives? Isn't it counterintuitive to ingest this overly processed, artificial food when I'm in such a volatile state and my body only needs what's essential and healthy? It also seems strangely comedic that I'm given no less than five different laxatives and medicines to aid my digestion and keep things moving through my body, yet the hospital food contains probably a quarter of the daily fiber a normal person needs. Why not ease up on the laxatives and feed me some extra broccoli or kale? I realize a fruit smoothie is probably more expensive than fake chocolate milk, but if it reduces my need for all those medicines, I'll bet it is actually more cost-effective in the long run—not to mention that it would taste a lot better than this fortified strangeness.

I ask the nurse to pour out the milk and place the empty carton with my belongings. This health shake has given me a lot to think about, and I want to come back to it as I work to better understand this process of rehab into which I've been thrust.

A few minutes later, Dr. Scott enters the room and begins our daily conversation, which covers every aspect of my rehab. Dr. Scott has been in charge of my rehab since I arrived in Vallejo. He meets regularly with Rick, the OTs, and anyone involved with me, to direct my care. Unlike Dr. Johnson, who despite her dire prognosis, imparted a somewhat positive and encouraging spirit in our one meeting, Dr. Scott is stern, blunt, and stoically grim in his dealings with me. He has told me more than once that the injury "is what it is," and that I should adapt to it as soon as possible and avoid getting my hopes up. I wonder if his imminent retirement, which he has mentioned many times, is the main cause for his rigid and seemingly outdated perspective on my injury and recovery.

Between the nurses emptying the bag of urine attached to my catheter and my mother peppering Dr. Scott with questions—which, to his credit, he always patiently answers—the room is a mini hub of activity.

"I'm going to order another round of blood tests for you today," Dr. Scott says monotonously.

"But I've had so many blood tests recently. Do I really need another one?" I glance at my junkie forearms, dotted with blue dots from the repeated needle plunges I've endured.

"The fever you've had since your surgery just isn't going away. I'm worried that your body is reacting badly to something, and that's why the fever keeps coming back at night. Those blood tests were all for different things, so we have to do more to monitor you and make sure we're not missing anything."

Maybe my body is reacting badly to all those laxatives you guys gave me, I wonder sarcastically to myself. I sigh as I struggle to remember the last time I had a fever. It must have been elementary school.

Then I see her out of the corner of my eye.

This time, Nancy is sitting comfortably behind Dr. Scott, just out of the nurses' way, but very much inside my room. I have no idea how long she's been there or what she's heard, but I immediately feel embarrassed. She remains there for the rest of our conversation, and Dr. Scott looks a bit surprised when he turns around to leave and sees her there.

The door was open, yes, but that doesn't mean anyone has the right to come in and listen to a private discussion between a patient and doctor. This has gone too far. I feel my anger growing exponentially with each breath. I glance at the clock and see that I have only a few minutes before my first session of the day. I look back at Nancy and wonder if she will give me a meaningful explanation.

"Hi, Arash, I just wanted to pop in and say hello," she says. "I'm looking forward to seeing you at the informational session tomorrow afternoon. I told you about it, right?"

"Yes, you did. More than once." I grit my teeth.

"Okay, great. See you then, if not before!" Before I have a chance to acknowledge my seething frustration, the nurse darts over to finish getting me dressed, and Nancy disappears.

***

The next day comes, and with it, a surprise two-day visit from my aunt, who has flown in from North Carolina. She asks if it's okay for her to accompany me to my therapy sessions that day. I'm excited to see her and explain that she's more than welcome to join the oh-so-joyous routines of an inpatient neurological rehab hospital.

At three o'clock sharp, my aunt and I head to the informational session entitled Living with Spinal Cord Injury. It comes as no surprise that Nancy is at the door, ready to excitedly usher us into the room where the session is being held. As we are getting settled, a nurse steps in to notify Nancy that the other three expected attendees can't make it. The only other person there is a balding man in his fifties, whom I've seen many times in the PT gym. He, too, sits in a wheelchair, but I've seen him walking around the gym and know that he's being discharged tomorrow. The hospital requires every patient to attend an informational session for his or her type of injury as part of physical and occupational therapy. We are both here as a formality, or so it seems.

Nancy begins by recounting her own injury, which occurred in her early twenties. "There were very few opportunities for rehabilitation back then," she says, "and the predominant attitude was that if you had a spinal cord injury, you were lucky if you could lead any sort of independent life. There was no discussion of regaining function because that wasn't an option."

I snicker when I hear this because it seems that little has changed in this regard.

As she goes through the rest of her story—much of which I've already heard in our previous interactions—my attitude toward her softens a bit. She has fought hard to prove she could live independently, to have a family and raise a daughter. I tell myself I shouldn't have been so critical of her and that maybe she does have a good perspective to share.

She moves on from her past to tell us about how much she enjoys her role at the hospital. "Now they've hired me to be here and act as a resource for all of you!" she exclaims. "These days, there are a lot of different opportunities for people in wheelchairs, so you shouldn't feel limited in any way."

I look over at the balding man-who-doesn't-really-need-a-wheelchair, and he smiles confidently, knowing this doesn't apply to him. *Lucky bastard*, I think. By next week, he'll likely be walking up and down stairs or playing golf, and this entire session will seem like ancient history. *What I would give to be in his shoes...* Maybe being overweight and balding and in my fifties would be worth it not to have paralysis.

"I could go on longer, but I guess I'm out of time," Nancy says. "Any questions?"

Balding man is already halfway out the door by the time I snap out of my daydream, and before I know it, Nancy is right up in my face. "Have you thought about what kind of wheelchair you're going to get?" she demands.

"Um... no. It's not what I want to think about—" I start to say.

But she cuts me off. "Well, you should think about it! It's important to figure out how to customize your wheelchair. There are so many cool options out there."

My newfound sympathy toward her is fading fast as I try to fend her off. "Yeah, like I was saying," I mutter, "I don't know much about it and I don't really want to—"

Again, she rides right over what I'm saying: "I've got tons of info you could check out! Look, I've got the catalogs for all the major manufacturers. I can go over them with you." She grabs one from the large stack on her lap, but it slips out of her hand and falls to the ground. "Oops, there it goes. I'm used to dropping things. This tenodesis isn't the best."

"Teno-? Tenodesis? What do you mean?"

"Yes, tenodesis. You'll become familiar with it, too. It's where you use your wrist to help you grip something because you can't use your fingers. See, if I want to hold something in my hand, I snap my wrist up and it helps me grab things. This is going to be useful for you, too!"

I've never heard of this tenodesis because my OTs have seen small but consistent improvements and have encouraged me to keep working on improving my hand function. I took that so much to heart that I'm still carrying the same red squeeze ball from the ambulance ride and John Muir Trauma Center with me throughout the day, constantly trying to strengthen my fingers. "I've played music since I was four-years-old, most recently guitar, and I'm dying to get my hands back to the point where I can play again," I try to explain.

Nancy gives me a puzzled look. I think it's the first time she's actually heard what I've said, and the first time she is responding to me directly: "Considering you're likely not going to play again, don't get too sad about it. For me, it was hard to accept that my hands were so damaged, but I got used to it. Just know that if the function doesn't come back, you'll learn to live without it. We're adaptable creatures, after all!"

She picks up the catalog, flips the pages in front of my increasingly tense face, and starts to go through each section. She points at the photos and describes in detail the benefits of one feature over the next. I tell myself that she must have worked at a car dealership at some point.

"Check out these wheels," she says. "When you roll, they light up so you can be seen at night! You should definitely get these."

After twenty more minutes of her excitedly describing every possible wheelchair accessory, and me barely nodding, I finally get a word in. "Nancy, my insurance refuses to pay for a wheelchair. I wish I didn't even need it, and I think it's ridiculous they won't provide the very thing I need to leave the hospital, but I've appealed and fought with them, and they absolutely say no. I'm going to have to pay for it out of pocket, so I don't think I'll be able to customize it. I'll just get the necessities, keep it pretty basic. And that's it."

Her response is quick and unmeasured: "Yeah, I hear you, but it's your chair! It's going to be a part of your life now, so you should give it some flair to reflect your personality. Look, there are so many colors to choose from. You don't have to put color all over the chair; you could just add a little splash and personality to some of the smaller parts. Make yourself stand out a bit. Look, you can get tiger stripes if you want!"

I've consciously made an effort for many years not to get too angry, and especially not to act upon my anger. I've come a long way since my younger days, when my temper was shorter and more likely to show itself. I hated that side of myself, so I decided I would do everything I could to handle frustration and anger in a mature, composed way. However, in this moment, it's taking everything I have not to lash out at Nancy. I'm not certain how to explain to her that me being in a wheelchair in the first place is as much standing out as I would ever want. And I don't need light-up wheels or tiger stripes on the frame to project my personality into the world. Her words go on repeat in my head: *"It's going to be a part of your life now."* She has no idea how damaging that statement is to me. I want nothing to do with a wheelchair—not now, not ever—and I've tried to convey that to her as subtly as I can, but to no avail.

Anger builds up inside me. Anger toward Nancy for being so insensitive and clueless. Anger toward the wheelchair that I'm asked to be excited about. Anger toward the hospital and the PTs and the doctors, and to everyone who repeatedly tries to tell me what I will be capable of doing in the future, as if that's predetermined. Anger toward my coworker, whose apartment I was trying to get into when I climbed up that balcony and started this entire nightmare. Anger toward everyone who has come to visit me and support me, because somehow their care, and my need for it, are a confirmation of this devastating situation, and I want nothing to do with it.

I take a deep breath, and with all my willpower, hold off the tempest overflowing inside me as I look her in the eyes. "I'll think about it, Nancy."

I look at my aunt, who has been silently observing all of this, and hope she has picked up on my cue that it's time to go. She nods in acknowledgment.

But Nancy doesn't stop. She has literally cornered me with her wheelchair so I can't escape without having her move first. "So, what kinds of home adaptations are you going to make?"

I choke down my rage and sigh loudly. "Home adaptations? I have no idea. I don't even know where my home is right now."

She looks confused. "Oh, I thought you were going to move into your parents' house in Berkeley. That's what the social worker has been discussing with them. Is that right?"

It stuns me that she would be privy to these interactions. And this isn't the first time I've seen that conversations between a patient or family members and members of the medical staff are not treated as confidential, as I had assumed they would be. I want to confront her about that, but first I have to address the mistaken assumption I feel she is making, "That's what's being discussed right now," I say. "I suppose that's where I could be going. I mean, nothing has been decided yet. The only thing I know for certain is that I can't go back to my third-story apartment in San Francisco."

She nods in agreement at my last point. "Of course not."

Then I confront her as calmly as I can: "But, Nancy, how did you know about the discussions with the social worker?"

She's taken aback, and slightly on the defensive. "Oh, I'm an employee of the hospital and this specific department, so I try to keep up with everyone's respective situation. That way I know how best to offer my help." It has become crystal clear to me that there is no way in which Nancy can help me, but short of slugging her, it seems I have no means to stop her. She continues, "That's why I was asking about home modifications. There are so many ways to modify a home for your new situation. They can do anything these days! There are lifts, elevators, ramps, and all kinds of changes to make the house more comfortable for you."

I think of my parents' small, creaky, craftsman home, which stood through the massive 1906 earthquake and the entire twentieth century, and I snicker at the thought of those narrow doorways, noisy stairs, and funky compartments being destroyed for some grotesque wheelchair lift.

Nancy is excited again, talking rapidly, and still unaware of my lack of interest and pending eruption. "I'll give you an example. I keep a bunch of cordless landline phones around the house. You know why? Because I don't always have my cell phone on me, and when I fall out of my chair onto the ground, I want to know there's a phone nearby I can use to call for help. That's just one trick I've learned, but there are many others I'm happy to share with you."

At this point, my stomach is churning from holding down my rage. I have to get out of there, or I won't be responsible for what happens next. "Nancy," I say, speaking distinctly in an effort to make sure I still sound polite. "I appreciate your offer to help, but right now, the only thing I can think about is my body and how to deal with everything that's happening. I'm still trying to sort out all the changes in me physically, so I'm not thinking about home adaptations or wheelchairs. I just don't have it in me to deal with that. I hope you can understand that. Can I go now?"

Evidently, my last four words are the only ones that Nancy hears. "Oh, of course!" she exclaims. "Here, just take these brochures with you."

My aunt reluctantly takes the stack of papers from Nancy and wheels me out the door.

***

The following day, I head to physical therapy, and as I wait for Rick to finish with his a client, I catch his eye.

"Be right with you, buddy," he mouths to me.

I nod as I slump lower into the wheelchair and allow my cumbersome neck collar to dig into my chest.

Rick and I pick up where we left off the previous day, working on pushing through with my arms to lift my hips off the table from a seated position and maintain my stability. Rick was ecstatic to see how much control I had when I first did this exercise and wants me to build off that momentum now. But within a few pushes, I lose my balance and tumble forward into him. I try again, and this time fall to the side. It's only due to Rick's attentiveness that my right ear doesn't slam into the table.

He grabs my shoulder and hoists me back up to sitting. "Whoa there. You were doing really well with this yesterday. You feeling okay?"

"Yeah. I'm fine," I say quickly. "Let's try it again."

I get through two more attempts before I lose my balance again, this time to the left.

Rick's gentle eyes are wide with concern now. "That was a close one, Arash. What's going on? Do you have pain anywhere?"

I try to look at him, but my vision is suddenly flooded with tears. All of those walls I constructed to hold off my frustration during yesterday's conversations with Nancy come crumbling down in a split second.

Rick listens to me patiently as I recount my exchanges with her. I explain all the interactions she imposed on me; her unsolicited advice; her habit of never asking me what I might want from her, if anything. My tears keep flowing as I recount all the details of the previous afternoon: the brochures; the light-up wheels; her proclamations of my "new situation"; how she held me captive for more than half an hour after the informational session ended, until I had to beg her to move aside and let me exit. I tell him that my aunt and I spent the whole afternoon going over the experience, trying to make sense of why someone with so little social awareness or emotional sensitivity would not only have access to read my files and know the details of my rehab, but would actually be paid to do so. I continue sobbing as I ask him why she, or anyone for that matter, would be allowed to roam around the hallways and approach me during my therapy sessions.

As my eyes finally start to dry out, Rick puts a hand on my shoulder. I notice him fighting off tears of his own. "Arash, you're the hardest-working person I've worked with in this place, hands down. I know how much you must be struggling with your injury, yet you show up here everyday and give it your all. We're all impressed with your drive and commitment to get better. It's plastered all over your face. I'm sorry about this whole experience, I really am. I'm going to figure something out for you. This is the first day I've seen you struggle so much with your therapy, and if Nancy has caused you to get to this point, then something needs to be done. I'm on it, buddy."

The next morning, as I'm about to get wheeled out of my room to see the neuropsychologist, Rick pops in and politely asks the nurse to let him take me to that meeting.

We wander down a couple of hallways, and once we're alone, he stops pushing the wheelchair and squats down in front of me. "Arash," he says, "as of this morning, you won't be seeing much of Nancy. She's not allowed to come into your therapy sessions, she's not going to talk to your family, and she knows she can't interact with you anymore. I was crushed when I saw you like that yesterday, and I knew I had to do something. I hope you don't think it's too extreme, but I think this is what you want, right?"

I smile from ear to ear and nod.

7.

Brita

It's the end of my third full week of rehab in Vallejo, and I'm settling into what has become a familiar routine. After each day of shuttling back and forth between the physical therapy gym, the occupational therapy room (where I work on my hands), and the other obligatory educational sessions (where I am taught the many aspects and complications of life with a spinal cord injury), I have a few quiet minutes in the late afternoon to rest in bed before the nurses arrive to perform their evening duties. I am particularly tired today from all the exercises I did earlier so when I see the phone call from my mother, I struggle to reach over and slide the touchscreen open with my knuckle to answer.

"Arash jaan, Brita just got here. She's going to come with us to the hospital, and we're bringing dinner for us all to enjoy. Hope you have an appetite!"

"Oh my god! That's great. I didn't know if she was going to come today or tomorrow. Okay, I'll see you guys in a while."

As soon as I hang up, I realize that aside from a short interaction with my father months ago, today is the first time Brita has met my parents. I'm disappointed that I wasn't there when she arrived. And now she has had to coordinate with them to get a ride to my present hospital home. I know how warm, easygoing, and welcoming my parents are, but I can't help but think that it's not an ideal situation for Brita. Who wants to meet her boyfriend's parents without her boyfriend present?

As I glimpse the catheter tube leading to the attached plastic bag full of urine hanging below my bed and feel the bulky neck brace and flowery hospital gown, I'm reminded of my pathetic state. Even though I've had the incredible fortune of having visitors every single day, I've never really cared about my appearance or how vulnerable I must seem to all of them, but all of a sudden I'm very aware of everything.

It's been over two months since Brita and I stood outside my apartment building on a foggy San Francisco morning, embraced each other eye to eye, and kissed goodbye. The memory of it is all too vivid, yet feels so far away in some respects. She was on her way to Lebanon for the summer for an Arabic language immersion program, the final requirement of her Master's program in international policy studies, and although I wasn't going to see her for a long time, I was already scheming how I would convince my new job to allow me to take all of my yet-unearned vacation time to travel to Beirut and visit her.

Now, thinking back to that last time I saw her in person, to the last conversation that didn't involve hospitals and medical reports and nurses in the background, it all seems bizarre. I feel like I'm living a completely different life, and at times like I'm barely living at all. But this has been my reality for the last month and a half, and knowing that within an hour the woman of my dreams, the person I fell in love with before this tragedy occurred, is on her way to see me terrifies as much as it excites me.

***

Brita and I first met on a blind date three months before she left for Lebanon. Not an online version, but a good ol' fashioned setup. My buddy called me and said his friend's wife—whom I had met briefly twice at large group gatherings and whom I barely knew—wanted to introduce me to her "tall, brilliant, athletic blonde friend who spoke Arabic," and asked if I'd be interested. I had been single for almost five years, casually dating here and there, but never too excited about the women I met. Apparently, Brita lived two hours south of me, in the quiet coastal town of Monterey. She was deep in her final semester of grad school, and had friends in San Francisco, and thus would inevitably be in my neck of the woods at some point. So when this opportunity came up, I figured I had nothing to lose. I might as well meet this girl for a beer, and if nothing came of it, she would go back to Monterey and I would go back to my social life of friends and family, which kept me plenty busy.

On a Saturday afternoon in March, Brita and I made plans to meet at a lively beer garden. I told my roommate to keep me posted on his plans so that if I were to want to escape, I could still meet him for dinner. "I'm sure she's perfectly nice, but I'm not expecting to fall in love or anything, so chances are I'll see you later," I said confidently.

"No problem bro," he said as I walked out the door to meet Brita. "I'll text you in a couple hours and see how you're doing."

I rode my bike down to the beer garden and locked it casually to a lamppost, virtually guaranteeing that I wouldn't stay long or let the night get too crazy, as that would mean subjecting my primary mode of transportation to the expert bike thieves of San Francisco. After waiting fifteen minutes for Brita and considering the very real possibility of her standing me up, I made a phone call and told myself that if Brita didn't show up by the time my conversation was done, I would likely call it quits and leave. A few minutes later, a striking blonde with piercing blue eyes stepped out of a car and walked straight toward me.

"So are you gonna keep talking on your phone or are you here to actually meet me?" she said confidently.

I couldn't help but feel slightly bewildered, amused, and surprisingly attracted to this girl, who was basically calling me out, even though *she* had been the one to show up twenty-five minutes late to our date. I hung up the phone and the adventure began.

***

I can hear my mother's voice describing the layout of the floor to Brita as they round the corner down the hallway by the nurse's station. I like keeping the door to my room open; hearing the mundane sounds of the neurological rehab unit is better than feeling cut off from everyone and everything. Not to mention that I have come to enjoy the twelve-second audible preview of anyone who is coming to visit me as they make their way from the elevator to my temporary abode.

They walk into the room, and Brita's face glows with a bright smile. "Hiiiiiiii! I missed you so much," she says as she leans down, maneuvers around my neck brace, and embraces me.

"It's so great to see you," I whisper, holding back my tears. "I can't believe you're actually here. You had to come all the way across the planet to see me like this..."

I call the nurse to help me transfer out of bed and into the wheelchair so we can go outside to the courtyard, which is where I spend nearly all my free time. I don't think the nurses are used to patients wanting to be out and about as much as I am, especially in the evening, when most have retired to their rooms and are watching TV or sleeping. I've gotten to know all of the nurses, and Lulu is one of my favorites. She is sweet, funny, and supportive, yet always slightly admonishing and authoritative in her thick Filipino accent.

"You always going out there! You sure you're not too tired? Maybe better if you stay in bed, no?" she says as she helps me out of bed.

"Nah, I'd rather be outside. The fresh air and sun are what I need. This room is too depressing." I reach for Brita's hand as I get into the wheelchair. "Lulu, I want to introduce you to my... um... she's um... this is Brita." After not seeing her for over two months, I'm tentative about how I refer to Brita. I don't want to make any assumptions about our relationship.

"She's very beautiful, Arash! You're a very lucky guy!" She shakes Brita's hand energetically, adjusts my catheter, and walks out the door.

Outside, my mom and dad pull out numerous Tupperware containers full of incredible homemade Persian food, and we begin to feast. I never expected Brita's first taste of my mother's cooking would be on a flimsy paper plate in a hospital courtyard, but it will have to do. My injury has destroyed my once-insatiable appetite so that now I struggle to find myself completely hungry, but the smells of khoresht-e-bademjoon (eggplant and chicken stew), kookoo sabzi (baked herbs, vegetables, and egg), and tadig (crispy, semi-burnt basmati rice from the bottom of the pot) make my mouth water. My mom offers Brita a few slices of raw onion to accompany the food, and I expect her to politely decline, as nearly all non-Persians do when encountering this not-so-common eating habit we have. I've had friends ask me why in the world we would corrupt our taste buds with the stinging bite of raw onions. I've had ex-girlfriends call me out and refuse to come near me after I ate Persian stew with plenty of raw onion. But to the surprise of my family and me, Brita not only accepts but dives right in and chomps down on the onion after taking a bite of food, matching what we do. I knew this girl was amazing every time I spent time with her, but she has just scored major points in my book. My mom gives me a quick smile, which I assume to mean, *How the hell did you find this sweet, brilliant, beautiful blonde girl from Minnesota who munches on raw onions like us?*

When dinner is over and the late summer sun has set, my family pack up to go home. Every night since I left the ICU, one of my parents has curled up in the glorified airline seat next to my bed and spent the night at the hospital. My cousin, who's home from college, and my uncle, who's practically my third parent and with whom I've been very close my entire life, have given them a few nights off, but most of the time, it's been one of them. But tonight, Brita insists she wants to stay with me.

As always, it takes more than an hour for the nurse to help me brush my teeth, change, and get ready for bed. When I finally get there, I'm overwhelmed with the simultaneous excitement about having time with Brita and anxiety about the interaction I'm about to have with her.

"I can't believe your parents have been sleeping in this chair every night," she says as she spreads out the sheet and reclines the chair flat, which is barely long enough for an average-size person to lie down, with his or her legs dangling off the end.

"I'm so happy you're here. It still seems unreal to me. I was sitting out on that courtyard Skyping you, and now here you are—from across the planet to this awful hospital."

She sits down on the bed, awkwardly avoiding the handrails, my catheter, and the other computer wires so she can be right next to me. "I can't believe this happened to you, Arash. I was sick to my stomach when

I found out. I couldn't do anything for three days. I contemplated leaving my program and coming back here to be with you, but—"

"But thankfully you didn't. That program was the last part of getting your Masters! Of course you had to stay and finish. And you wouldn't have missed much, just me in a slightly worse state than I am right now," I snicker.

"You're still just as handsome as I remember you." She smiles and squeezes my hand.

I try to smile back, but tears are welling up in my eyes. "Brita... this injury is really bad. Much worse than anything I've ever known."

"I know. You've kept me up to date with everything so far, with all the stupid prognoses they've given you. And of course I've had plenty of time to do my own reading and research."

"I know you have, babe, but... it's just that... this is gonna be *really* tough." I'm having a hard time finding the right words, but I continue. "I think a lot of what these doctors say is complete bullshit, but what I do know is that things are going to be really hard for a while. This injury has destroyed me in so many ways. It's not just my lower body and the loss of control. It's everything! And every time I ask them about how soon I'll get better and about my recovery, they tell me not to have many expectations and to do my best to adapt to the situation. I'm so sick of it."

"I know you are, sweetie. It's such a shame how they're handling this."

"You know what Dr. Scott said to me today, after he found out you were coming and I told him a bit about you? I had asked about acupuncture and some of the other approaches for regaining function, and he laughed them off. His exact words were 'Don't waste your time with those methods or approaches. There's no evidence that any of that stuff will help you at all. The best thing for you and your girlfriend is to go on a vacation. Go on a cruise, relax, enjoy your time together.'"

"Really? That's what he said? Go on a *cruise*?"

"I kid you not. As if I'm in any condition to do anything like that, or that the first thought on my mind is to relax. I couldn't believe it. He paid no attention to what I actually wanted, he just said his own thing."

"I can't believe that. Doesn't he know that your focus is on recovery? Hasn't he seen how hard you're trying to get better?"

"This is the nature of what I'm dealing with. It's the paradigm in which these people work. I think he's spewing the same stuff he learned in medical school forty-five years ago. As if things haven't changed, and there aren't any new approaches and ideas."

"That's shocking, and disappointing," she says.

I've digressed from my original intention with the conversation, so I rein it back in. "Brita, I've been wanting to bring this up with you. I feel terrible for what I've put you through, for giving you all that stress while you were at your language program, for making you cut your trip short and keeping you from exploring like you wanted to, like *we* were planning to." Just days before my injury, I had booked a ticket to Lebanon, and we were planning to spend two weeks together traveling through the area. "Obviously, I feel an incredible connection with you, I have since we met. And even though we only had a couple of months to get to know each other before this accident, I knew that our bond was unique and that I had really strong feelings for you."

"I know that. I feel all the same for you."

"I know, but the truth is my life is going to be really hard for a long time. I have a sense of it, but even my own expectations are way off from what it actually may be. I'm in a pretty tough situation." I sigh and glance away for a moment before I look back up at her patient, loving blue eyes. "Now that you've seen me like this, now that you know just how real this all is, if you decide you don't want anything to do with this, then I'm not going to hold it against you. I don't expect you to want to deal with this at all. In fact, I expect that you don't, and so I will never say a bad thing about you or think poorly of you if you tell me right now that you want out. This is your chance."

Brita fixes her eyes upon me with an unmistakable determination. "NO. WAY. I'm not going anywhere."

"Didn't you hear what I said?" I say with confusion. "You can go. No questions asked. I won't be mad. I promise."

"Yes I heard you, and yes I understand, but I'm not leaving you. I care about you so much, and if you have to go through this, then I'm going through it with you."

I'm overcome with a sense of relief, yet I can't deny that I'm slightly surprised. I knew Brita and I both had deep feelings for each other, and although we hadn't yet used the "L" word, it was inevitable. But I had expected more of a back and forth. I thought she would consider making a clean break from my horrific reality, and I was trying to make it easier for herself. She just finished graduate school after all, in a field she loves and she is embarking on a career path that could take her anywhere in the world. The world is her oyster.

By contrast, my world is an imminent discharge from the hospital, a move-in with my parents, and the daunting task of trying to survive through each day without making matters worse for myself. I hold Brita's gaze silently, giving her one last chance to rid herself of me.

But she doesn't flinch. She gently strokes my head with her fingers and smiles at me. "I'm not going anywhere. Like I just said."

As she leans in to hug me, I explode into tears. I grasp onto her shoulders, pull her close to me, and decide that I never want to let go.

She lies down next to me, and we hold each other quietly as the beeps and hums and hushed voices of the hospital hallways fade away, and the warm serenity of a newly validated and deepening love envelops me and lulls me to sleep.

8.

Valentine and Jana

I open my eyes with a startle and am confused by my surroundings. As I glance around the room and notice the get well cards atop my childhood dresser and the posters on the otherwise blank white walls of the unfamiliar room, my eyes settle on the wheelchair next to my bed. I'm immediately aware of where I am. I realize that this is the morning I will meet the new physical therapist who will come to my home and help me do therapy here.

It's been almost a week since I left the hospital to "live my new life," as the hospital staff referred to it, in a home that isn't home. Every time I remember that day the social worker informed me of my discharge date and how I ended up in this strange, alien apartment next to the train tracks, I get angry all over again.

***

I was only days into rehab in Vallejo when Debbie, the generally friendly yet perennially overwhelmed and neurotic social worker, popped into my room to tell me the hospital had decided they would send me home from the hospital at the end of August, less than a month from that moment. I was confused that in such a short time following my operation and with my body in such an incredibly vulnerable state, they were already able to know, and plan, for my departure date. Wouldn't they need to give me some time to do rehab and see how much I could progress? Shouldn't the discharge date be determined *after* I'd had an opportunity to strengthen my body and be more ready to transition out of the hospital and back into the real world?

Needless to say, Debbie's announcement resulted in a mad panic to figure out where I would live and who would help with my daily needs. With a laundry list of physical complications and challenges—the most obvious and significant being the wheelchair—I was going to need round-the-clock care. My parents, whose lives had been in limbo since they got that call from the ICU, told me not to worry; they would do anything and everything necessary to help. They were the two most caring, loving, supportive and self-sacrificing people imaginable, and they had already practically moved mountains to raise me, so it was not a surprise they would step up in this way. Still, I was overwhelmed with guilt at the prospect of upending their lives so completely.

Unfortunately, the century-old house they had owned and lived in for the last fifteen years was absolutely *not* accessible, with its sixteen steps leading to the front door, narrow doorways, and cramped bathroom. Debbie and the hospital administration, who had been slow to respond to most of my requests, were surprisingly quick and resourceful when it came to connecting my parents with contractors who could install a wheelchair lift and make other adaptations to their home. That, I realized, was why Nancy had made such a big point about home renovations. I suppose I shouldn't have been surprised that any communications that would expedite the process of getting me *out* of the hospital and out of their care would be given highest priority, but at the time, I was.

My parents were given quotes for the many alterations they would have to make. However, with my medical insurance refusing to pay for the sky-high costs, the option of living in their home quickly became impossible. As a result, they begged the hospital to extend my stay in rehab. They wrote to the hospital and insurance company, explaining their challenges and asking how it was possible that the full responsibility for care of someone with as traumatic an injury as mine could be passed on to them. They cited the past practices of hospitals for people with spinal cord injuries, as well as the lengthy stays and extended months of rehab. But the insurance company rejected all of it.

To them, keeping someone like me in a rehab setting and providing extended physical rehabilitation was too expensive, even unnecessary. To keep costs manageable, they argued that the hospital and insurance provider had to get the patient as functional as possible, as quickly as possible. That meant booting them out of the hospital and "back" to their lives, regardless of whether they felt ready for the move.

As my parents and I researched recovery from a traumatic spinal cord injury, the results we found were insubstantial and convoluted. Any rare cases of dramatic recoveries usually happened over the course of many years. To complicate matters, unlike a more simple injury, such as a torn *anterior cruciate ligament* (ACL) or broken bone, there was no way to predict if or how someone would recover from a spinal cord injury. Even people who broke the exact same vertebrae and sustained similar spinal cord injuries could have radically different outcomes. Therefore, the approach of the current medical system—to which I was now subject—was to emphasize accepting and adapting to my new circumstances instead of maximizing recovery.

As a result, practically all my physical therapy was geared toward getting me to be functional in day-to-day activities: sitting up without falling, transferring in and out of the wheelchair, moving around in bed, strengthening my upper body just enough to make up for the lack of function in the rest of my body. "Everything we do with you has to be justified with respect to a specific function," they would say. "Most importantly, we have to get you to be *as independent as possible.*"

This phrase, uttered far too often, was supposed to be the means of motivating me. But I couldn't wrap my head around the fact that the system was predicated on the belief that I should move forward with the assumption I wouldn't improve at all, and that therefore, I must spend my efforts adapting to my current body instead of trying to regain function.

Every time I brought up my larger goals of getting back on my feet and strengthening my entire body, the doctors and therapists gave me the same quizzical look Rick gave me on that first day of rehab. They politely dismissed me.

"I'm not delusional," I would tell them. I understood the magnitude of my injury and how compromised my body now was. I had gone from being in the best shape of my life to losing twenty-five pounds and barely being able to push myself in a wheelchair. I had no idea how I would regain the function I so desperately wanted, but I knew I had to try. It was the most important thing in the world to me now. Every day I was frustrated and angry with the therapists and doctors for their approach, but I knew I had to start somewhere, that the long path to recovery would reveal itself over time, and that for now I had to listen to their suggestions and work as hard as I could doing everything they asked of me.

Once it was clear that my discharge date from the hospital wasn't going to change—and that come hell or high water, my family was going to take on the full burden of my care, and their current home was not an option—my parents scrambled to find a feasible alternative. At one point, my father asked Debbie what would happen if we still hadn't found a viable place to live on the day of my discharge.

She offered a half-sincere apology and basically said it wasn't the hospital's problem anymore. "Sucks for you guys," was the sixth-grader's version of her response.

Luckily, just days before my discharge, my parents signed a six-month lease for an apartment in a modern building with an elevator, only minutes from their house. They had no idea how they would pay their mortgage and deal with the additional astronomical cost of rent in one of the most expensive real estate markets in the country, but there was no other option. And so it was that, just five days after my thirty-first birthday, my seven-week stay in three different hospitals came to an end, and I came "home" to this new apartment and a dramatically different life.

***

It's a few minutes past 10 am when the front door to the apartment swings open and a flustered woman scrambles in and greets me. "I'm here to do your homecare physical therapy. My name is Valentine. Is there a table where I can put my stuff down? And we can get started?"

She is so weighed down with the numerous bags slung over her shoulders, seemingly vomiting their contents from the many unzipped pockets, that it looks more like she's on her way to the airport for a month-long business trip than coming for a one hour session in my home. She's relieved as she drops all her belongings next to the dining table, but not before dozens of papers slide out of a folder and fall to the ground.

"Oops! Oh well, that's okay. I have to sort those papers out later anyway." She smiles awkwardly, pulls out a beat-up laptop that looks like it's from 1997 and crawls under the table to connect it to the outlet. "It doesn't work unless it's plugged into power," she explains, as if that would answer all the questions in my mind.

Wow, these insurance companies are really setting their employees up for success, aren't they? I think.

After a few more minutes of her shuffling through folders of papers, waiting for her computer to turn on, and pulling out and plugging in both her cell phones, she has the table looking like central command for a clandestine military operation. Valentine exhales deeply, then looks squarely at me for the first time. She's in her mid forties, with overgrown, curly, graying brown hair that swallows her ears. Her beady brown eyes are framed by thick black glasses that would get a seven-year-old on a playground multiple beatings a day. She has a subtle but noticeable French accent, which she tells me is from her childhood in Quebec.

A few minutes into the litany of health-related questions I've become so accustomed to answering, a ring goes off on one of her phones, but she silences it. Five minutes later, still mired in questions and furious box ticking, the phone rings again and she silences it. Then, as she is in the middle of tightening the blood pressure cuff on my arm, the ring goes off once more. Again she silences it.

After the seventh ring, I can't help myself any longer. "Umm, I think someone is trying to call you, Valentine. If you need to answer it, go ahead."

She looks up as if she's surprised I noticed the repeated ringing. "Oh, that's not a call. It's an alarm. It reminds me to be happy."

"And it goes off frequently?"

"Every five minutes. I've battled with depression for a while. Every time the alarm goes off, I try to think of being happy."

"So it continues all day? While you're working? Driving?"

"Yup, it helps." She smiles awkwardly and gets back to the paperwork.

It becomes clear from her questions and her puzzled expressions after each of my responses that Valentine has never worked with a spinal cord injury before. She admits that she actually has very little experience with neurological issues. "I've had a couple of stroke patients, but because of their advanced age, I didn't do anything beyond stretching and basic exercises with them. You'll have to teach me a bit about spinal cord injury."

"I'm still figuring it out myself. I've only been in this body for a couple of months, and everything feels so different from what it used to," I say.

A few minutes go by, she asks more questions and takes another measurement of blood pressure, and then she glances at her watch and jumps back into her more flustered state. "Oh shoot! I have to run to my next appointment. I'm sorry this visit had to be all paperwork and formalities. I promise next time we can get into some exercises. Don't worry, we will figure some things out." Then, with the same tornado in which she arrived, she throws together her papers, packs up her stuff, and heads out the door, bags swaying precariously on her shoulders and folders desperately trying to contain their contents.

Well, she was a character, I think to myself.

***

It's the next afternoon, and I'm waiting for the homecare occupational therapist to arrive. After my encounter with Valentine, who seemed ill-equipped for my challenges, I'm crossing my fingers that the OT may pleasantly surprise me, even though I'm preparing myself for any kind of wildcard.

This time, I'm greeted by a short, tan woman of about fifty-five, with bangs, shoulder-length hair, and a flowery blouse. Jana walks over to the same dining table that turned into Operation Valentine the day before, and sits down. She only has one bag, one phone, and one organized folder, and from what I can surmise, no happiness alarm. She takes my blood pressure, comments that it's very low, and begins asking me many of the same questions I answered yesterday about my health and condition.

Just as I'm about to fret that the entire hour will go to formalities once again, she scans me up and down and then settles her eyes on my face. "So, what do you want to work on?" she asks as she shrugs her shoulders.

"I thought *you* would be able to tell *me*," I reply, unable to hide my newfound frustration.

"Well, I read your file and am aware of what you did in the hospital. It said you were doing ice plunges and electrical stimulation with your hands, before doing finger dexterity work. Is that right?"

"Yes, yes that's right!" I become somewhat hopeful. "My hands improved quite a bit during my time at inpatient rehab. They're still really weak, but I liked everything I did there. I mean... the ice plunges were tough as hell, but I liked the sensation they gave me afterwards. I was assuming you'd continue where I left off at the hospital."

She takes my hands in hers and starts testing the strength of each finger, as well as my overall grip and wrist function. "So, your index finger and thumb are still pretty weak, huh?"

"I would say everything is weak. But yeah, they're quite a bit weaker than my pinkies and ring fingers. And the middle fingers are kinda halfway between the two," I say, acknowledging the strange symmetry of finger strength within my hands.

"How are you performing your everyday functions so far? Getting dressed, going to the bathroom, feeding yourself?" she asks as she stares at my hands.

"I need help with most things, so my parents are usually there for all that. Luckily, I can hold a fork or spoon well enough to eat, but I'm hoping that as I get stronger, I'll be able to do more. I left the hospital less than a week ago so I'm still getting used to all of this." I hope my last sentence registers a bit of empathy with her and kicks her into gear for continuing some of those very effective exercises I was doing in rehab. But I'm quickly proven wrong.

"It's very important that you get back to doing as many of your everyday functions as soon as possible, even if it means changing the way you do them," she says somewhat sternly. "The sooner you can adapt and become *as independent as possible,* the happier you will be." She has no idea how much of a nerve she has just struck.

"What do you mean by 'changing the way I do things?'"

"Oh, there are tools to help you achieve many of your everyday functions. It's really incredible. What are your primary functional goals?"

Functional goals? I repeat to myself. I've heard this song and dance routine before, having spent nearly two months in the hospital and become accustomed to the vernacular of doctors and therapists and their constant emphasis on adaptation. I decide to answer with the blunt candor I've developed in response to this approach: "I have one functional goal, and it's pretty straightforward. I want to recover as much function as I can. All other tasks will become easier if I'm able to regain more function."

She looks a bit bewildered, then jumps back into her previous statement, seemingly ignoring my rebellious claim. "Well, you should look at some of the tools that can help you with your everyday functions. For example, how do you prepare your meals? Did you cook before your injury at all?"

"Actually, yeah. I've been cooking since I was a kid. As a matter of fact, it's one of my passions, and I'd love to get my hands strong enough to cook again. But in the few days I've been home from the hospital, there has been so much to deal with that I honestly haven't been able to even think about trying to cook or do much in the kitchen."

"Why don't we start there? Maybe we can figure out how to make things easier for you to navigate the kitchen. There are lots of adaptive knives and cooking tools, mirrors you can install over the stove, and modifications you can make to the kitchen to make it work for your needs."

The sinking feeling of frustration hits me as I realize that, once again, my goals and desires are not being heard or addressed, and that the consistent emphasis on adaptation will drive the conversation and our work together. "We just moved to this apartment a couple weeks ago. We're not expecting to stay too long. It's just a temporary place my parents were forced to rent because their house isn't wheelchair accessible, so I'm not sure that making modifications to the kitchen is realistic," I explain. "Don't get me wrong, Jana, I'd love to be able to cook soon, but I'd rather focus on the progress I was making with my hands at rehab. Is there any way to do similar exercises here?"

Her friendly face turns sour and annoyed. "This is homecare OT; it's different from what you did at the hospital. I don't have an electrical stimulation machine, so I can't do that. As for the other tools you used, if you have something in the house, I can use that, but I don't have anything with me."

"So what do you usually do with people like me?"

"It's like I told you: I work on finding solutions to everyday tasks and on making life at home easier or smoother. I think, for you, the basics in the kitchen are a good start. I mean, what will you do if no one is around and you want to make yourself a sandwich or something?"

A sandwich?! Lady, that's the least of my problems, I think. I realize I'm likely going to lose this battle, especially since she is apparently supplied with a whole lot of nothing to help me so I decide to humor her. "Fine. Let's give it a shot."

I spend the next thirty minutes spinning the wheelchair around the narrow kitchen—since that's pretty much all I can do—watching her open drawers and cupboards. She pulls out various utensils and dishes, examines them briefly, then puts them back in their place. "Hmm, these plates are a bit far away for you to reach," she says. "Maybe you guys can move them somewhere closer for you?"

"Um, I can't even hold a plate right now."

"Oh, right. Okay. Maybe we can find a cutting board you could put on your lap? Then you could use that to put food on or make a sandwich or whatever."

Again with the sandwich. As I'm opening my mouth to tell her—to her likely dismay—that I'm not a big fan of sandwiches, she runs out of the kitchen and gets on her computer.

After entirely too many minutes of clicking and reading, she turns the laptop toward me and shows me the page. It's Amazon.com. "Here are some cutting boards that could work for you."

I scan the page, assuming she's explored some deep, dark corner of Amazon that I wouldn't have looked at, but everything I see there looks like a display case at Macy's. I glance at the search box and see that she typed in "cutting boards." My anger continues to build at this person who has just wasted nearly five minutes of the mere one hour a week she is due to spend with me on an Amazon search that would have taken me all of six seconds.

I take a deep breath, try to assure myself that she is here to serve some kind of semi-useful purpose, and continue to play her game. "So, is a cutting board or adaptive kitchen tool something my insurance will provide—you know, to 'make my life easier'?" I ask, repeating her phrase.

"Oh, no, no, no," she chuckles. "I can't order anything for you, and the insurance won't buy any of that. I can help you find the right thing, though! Maybe we should measure your lap to see what size cutting board would work best for you."

"I'm not sure if..."

Before I can get out the words to object, she glances at the clock. "Oh! Look at the time. Our hour is up. Okay, I'll call you about scheduling next week's appointment. Have a good week!"

And just like that, she's out the door. Once again, I'm left confused, frustrated, and defeated.

I struggle to make sense of the incredible drop-off in quality between the rehab therapists I worked with in the hospital, who always had a detailed plan of action and responded to my high energy with a liveliness and vigor of their own, and the two bumbling personalities I'm dealing with now. I realize there is more complexity to this health-care system I am now so intimately involved with than I ever knew. I wonder if the limitations of the therapists in the hospital were due to an outdated, unchanging paradigm under which the entire medical system operates. This is a system, after all, that financed the construction of a brand-new neurological rehab center and purchased some of the most innovative treadmills, as well as gait training devices with harnesses that could support most humans (and possibly even livestock animals). Yet all that equipment sat unused in the corner of the sparkling, shiny new gym.

My mother was overjoyed when she first saw that equipment because it validated the many hours of research she had done to learn about the most current assistive walking therapies. But when she asked the physical therapists why she never saw any patients using them, she was told the labor cost for using machines that required two or more therapists to operate for each patient was "unjustified" and "unnecessary." The PTs said there was plenty they could do one-on-one with patients, without the need of costly equipment.

In other words, why waste money on labor for using the machines for which the hospital spent hundreds of thousands of dollars, when they could just let them sit there and function as ornamental pieces for the gym? Why entertain the idea of progressive approaches to recovery, when it is more cost-efficient to take the easy way out by encouraging patients to tame their expectations and focusing their therapy on everyday functions, tasks, and adaptations?

Sarcasm aside, the expectations for improvement for patients with spinal cord injuries or other significant neurological conditions are minimal to none. The shortsightedness of the insurance companies is evident in their decision to refrain from providing more intensive care or therapy (such as the aforementioned gait training and treadmills that required more labor) that could improve the lives of these patients; restore more function and ease in their everyday lives; and reduce the likelihood of secondary complications, which were so common and so costly for insurance. But is there 100 percent empirical proof, with measurable outcomes and data points, that more therapy and exercise will lead to better outcomes? Probably not. Thus the operating paradigm of the insurance companies, hospitals, and rehab units has come to emphasize adaptation; to tame expectations; and to reject anything but the most minimal financial investment in labor, equipment, and therapy.

Put more simply, my experience shows me that rehab in the hospital was funded and is intended to get patients to reach the absolute minimal level of independence, so they basically aren't shitting their own pants or falling out of their wheelchairs. The hospital is spared the financial burden of keeping them under the care of nurses, doctors, and therapists by discharging them and passing their care off to their families and loved ones—if they are lucky enough to have that kind of support.

And so here I am now, out of the hospital's hair, less of a financial burden to the insurance company, in my parents' makeshift apartment, and dealing with the medical system's next phase of rehabilitation—which has introduced me to Valentine and Jana.

***

By the time Valentine comes back to the apartment for her second visit, a long week has passed, and I'm beyond antsy to find some kind of home routine to get myself moving. Our first interaction was odd and didn't exactly leave me very optimistic, but at this point, I really don't have any other options. It's best to try to make the most of my opportunity with Valentine and squeeze out the most I can from my one-and-only hour a week with her. I also realize that to do this, I'm going to have to get much more outspoken and direct about our time together.

Thankfully, Valentine is a bit more organized this time. After only two alarm happiness reminders on her phone, we are ready to get to work and do something beyond paperwork and Q&A.

She asks me what my goals are, and I instantly feel an unsettling in my stomach as I remember the many times in the hospital that I answered this question and struggled to find a good response. "Look, Valentine, I'm going to be straightforward with you. I know you probably operate under the same constraints as the PTs I encountered in rehab and are probably expecting to just help me 'adapt,' but my goals are way bigger than that. I want to get back on my feet and walk. That's my ultimate goal. I know I have to get stronger in a lot of ways, so whatever you can do right now to help me establish a good home routine would be my preference. Do you think you could help me in this way?"

"Arash, I've never worked with a spinal cord injury before and have limited experience with anything neurological, so really I have no expectations to work with!" She chuckles uncomfortably. "For better or for worse, I'm a blank slate and I'm happy to do my best to help you."

"Awesome. Let's give it a try."

"So what's something you need help with now?" she asks, with a newfound sense of initiative that I appreciate.

"One of the many struggles of having an injury that has completely taken away the control of my abs and core is that, from a lying down position in bed, I'm not able to sit up or roll to my side or stomach to change positions. Once I'm lying on my back, I'm basically like a face-up turtle in its shell, stuck and completely helpless. So far, my parents have been on call to yank me up from my wrists whenever I've needed to sit up. And thankfully, a couple days ago, a family friend donated an old hospital bed with grab bars on either side and a remote control that can raise and lower the top half of the bed. It's made things a bit easier, but I still feel really vulnerable lying in bed. Finding ways to move around and sit up would be really helpful."

"Hmm, okay. I might have some ideas."

To my surprise, Valentine comes up with a simple yet effective stretching routine to do first thing in the morning. It is intended to help me sit up and roll around in bed more successfully. Then she shows me how I can sweep my arm to one side, lean on the elbow, and use the momentum to push myself up to sitting on my own. She is resourceful enough to roll up a towel so my dad and I can use it to stretch my ankles, calves, and feet. It's not groundbreaking exercise, but it's enough to leave me with some homework and a routine to work with during the 167 hours a week when she isn't present.

***

The next time I see Jana, she picks up right where she left off—talking about sandwiches, adaptive knives, and the size of my lap. She's had time to make a note to herself about our titillating cutting board conversation and to remind herself to bring a tape measure. However, she didn't have time to do any of her expert Amazon.com research before she came. Of course, the first thing she does is jump onto her computer and begin her glacial scan through the website.

I interrupt her immediately, unable to stand this astounding display of ineptitude. "Jana, I think I can handle the online research. I'd like to use our time a little better." I contemplate lying and assuring her that my insatiable desire for sandwiches will be met with or without cutting boards on my lap.

She looks up from her laptop in surprise. "Oh, okay. What would you like to do instead?"

"I want to *strengthen my hands*!" I practically shout. "I thought I made this clear last time."

"My role as a homecare OT is to help you with daily functions and make tasks around the house easier. That's what I'm here to do."

"Yeah, I remember. You made that very clear last week."

"So, are there any functional goals around the house that you are struggling with that we can address?"

"Every function right now is a struggle! I can't put on my clothes. I can't button a shirt. I can't floss. I can't shave. I can barely brush my teeth. I can shampoo if I rub my fists on my hair, but not my open hands. And I kinda, sorta can wipe my own ass, but even that's not guaranteed!"

Her face implies that she has finally registered my frustration. "I get it. I can't imagine how hard it must be. So let's pick a couple of those things and work on them."

"I appreciate that," I say, practically in tears now. "But the common thread to all of it is to *get my hands stronger*. If I can regain and improve function in my hands, then all the things I mentioned will get easier, right? So why can't we do that? Aren't there any finger or hand stretches or strengthening exercises you can show me?"

"I can't think of much off the top of my head, but let me add that to my list for next time. For now, let's just try to work on some of your daily routine tasks, like you mentioned."

"You keep saying I have to give you functional goals to work toward, and that you'll help me practice those goals, right?"

"Yes! Exactly." She seems satisfied now.

"Okay, but doesn't that assume I'm only operating with my current level of function? I mean, suppose you teach me how to do these tasks or tell me about adaptive products to use. But if I get better, I won't need them. What then?"

She pauses for a moment, giving me a perplexed look. "From what I know, there's no indication of *if* or *when* you'll have any more function or get better. That's why we have to get you adjusted to your new life and doing as much as you can to be independent. That's why I'm looking for tasks for us to do together so I can help you accomplish them!"

My head sinks in defeat, and my voice drops. "I... I don't... I just don't get it. I know I'm going to get better. My hands improved a lot just in my time in rehab."

"Your hands may get better, but we need to adapt to the situation now. Let's examine some of your tasks together, okay? Maybe it will make you feel better to gain some independence and know that you can do some of these things."

I finally make peace with the fact that Jana will not be my saving grace for improving my hands. I concede to her, and spend the rest of the hour poking around the house and casually going through my bedroom and bathroom, quickly analyzing the various tasks of everyday living I took for granted for the first three decades of my life. It ends up being more talk than action, and mostly involves her asking me how I do a specific task, me showing her, and her making obvious suggestions or telling me about tools I should buy to ease these tasks. There is no talk about how to train my fingers and hands to improve enough to accomplish a given task, just discussion about adaptation to my current state.

I'm beyond dejected and frustrated when she gets back on her laptop and starts to browse through silicon hooks and straps and contraptions that attach to hindered hands like mine. I admit how impressive some of these inventions are, how much time and effort it must have taken to create a wrist harness with small hooks that helps someone button a shirt. But I'm upset, again, that my sixty measly minutes of therapy provided by my medical insurance is being wasted as I sit silently and watch someone else peruse Amazon.com slowly and inefficiently in front of me.

***

A new week begins, and I'm already strategizing how to maximize my time with each of my homecare therapists. I laugh at how pathetic I must be, looking forward so much to one paltry hour with each of them.

My visits with Jana have left me beyond frustrated, but I'm holding out hope for Valentine. She has at least shown a willingness to try.

In her subsequent visit, Valentine shows up, still flustered and disorganized, but with more information and ideas about how to strengthen my badly compromised body. She tells me about the research she's done on spinal cord injury and the things she's learned. Unlike her colleague, she went onto Amazon.com on her own time, and shows me printouts of push-up handles, yoga blocks, and other simple items I can find useful around the house.

We end up spending the hour effectively and creatively. Despite my initial apprehensions about Valentine and her incessant happiness alarm (which continues to light up her cell phone and ring at five minute intervals), I am pleasantly surprised. She has at least recognized my desire and drive to do anything and everything I can to improve my condition. And I appreciate her initiative to come up with ideas and solutions for my mobility and exercise within the home.

She's even gotten the powers that be to grant me a second hour of therapy with her every week. "I really had to fight hard to justify that seeing you for another hour would benefit you greatly, but I was able to convince them," she says with a smile.

The things you have to do to get two measly hours a week of physical therapy after you've suffered a life-altering injury, I think.

***

My third visit from Jana is uneventful and uninspiring. She brings up the sandwiches and cutting board again, and spends most of the hour shuffling about the apartment and describing all the modifications I should look into to increase my independence. After she's finished meticulously explaining the ways to remove drawers, knock down cabinets, and redesign the entire kitchen, I politely remind her that this apartment is a temporary home. I reiterate that we have no plan of staying here long term, and that my parents are still paying a mortgage on a house I can't live in, while also taking on the burden of this rental. I tell her I have no money to make any modifications, and insurance won't pay for any of it. Unless she knows of some financial grant, or a benevolent genie or a magical wand she can wave, everything she said is irrelevant.

"Ohhh, right. Well, at least you know what the options are for your future living situation, wherever it may be!"

I'm not amused. Our meeting doesn't even last the full hour this time, as Jana recognizes that I've lost all patience with her and there's little she can do to help.

She takes my blood pressure one more time, gives me a printout of Amazon links for more hand contraptions, and packs up her stuff. Then she concludes, "I've done what I can to help you with your functional tasks. If you think of any other specific functions you want to work toward, call the OT department, and they can try to schedule another homecare visit. Good luck with everything!"

With that, she scurries out the door, down the hallway, and out of my life.

9.

Don't Sweat It

It's a scorching hot morning in Berkeley—not unheard of in October, when a heat wave can provide a taste of summer warmth that is usually lacking in the cool and foggy months of June through August. I reach to the side of the bed and hook my two barely functional fingers around the loop of the controller that raises the upper half of the hospital bed up to sitting. Although I've been working on the exercises Valentine taught me, I'm still too weak to sit up on my own when I'm lying flat. The hospital bed is the easiest way for me to get out of that helpless position. My thumbs have little to no strength, so I grasp the controller between my palms and use my knuckles to hold the button, which slowly raises me to sitting.

Brita tiptoes into the bedroom and sees me rubbing the sleep out of my eyes. Because my bed is too small for both of us, and I have numerous middle-of-the-night wakeup calls—for my parents to turn me from side to side (to avoid bedsores) and so I can empty my bladder with an intermittent catheter—she has to sleep on the couch for those couple of nights a week that she spends here. Her transition from finishing graduate school to looking for a job has been turned upside down by my injury, which only adds to the tremendous guilt I feel over the impact I've had on so many around me. She has been struggling to find job opportunities while she tries to spend as much time as possible with me.

But on this morning, she is cheerful and excited. "It's so nice out! We should do something outside."

She knows my morning routine will take me at least two hours, so she calls in my dad to get the process started.

Like most people with spinal cord injuries, I've lost control of my bowel and bladder function, so what used to be a glorious two-minute routine now requires me to sit on the toilet for the time it would take to view a feature film. It's difficult to describe how frustrating and disheartening it is to be forced to have my own father put on a latex glove, insert a suppository, and manually stimulate my anus just so I don't implode from my own poop—which is a very real and dangerous consequence of my injury. It's awful, it's embarrassing, and it's become all-too normal. Follow that with a laborious process to roll around the bed to get dressed, and painstakingly slide on skin-tight pressure socks (to help keep my low blood pressure in check), and it's nearly noon by the time all the waste has been drained and pushed out of my body and I'm finally dressed and ready to head outside.

Brita and I pick up sushi and take it to the large regional park in the hills above Berkeley. I fight off the wave of nostalgia as we park the car at Inspiration Point, where I used to ride my bike with my dad on Sundays when I was in elementary school. I'm tempted to think about all the soccer games and barbecues I enjoyed here throughout my childhood and teenage years, but the haunting memories are too painful, and I push them away. I focus my attention on the present moment and try to convince myself that what I'm doing isn't that different from what I would do without this injury. As we spread out the plastic containers and soy sauce packets on the bench, I begin to appreciate this rare opportunity to enjoy lunch outside, in the sunshine and fresh air, with my lovely girlfriend.

It only takes a few minutes before I start to feel hot. I touch my head and face to check for sweat, but my skin is as dry as a weathered catcher's mitt. Not one bead of sweat. I stay there a bit longer, trying to focus on the spicy tuna and pickled ginger, only to find that my discomfort is almost unbearable. It's barely been six months since we met, but Brita already knows how much I love the sunshine. I never shy away from its bright, radiant light. So she knows something is a bit strange when I ask to move to the shade. She obliges me, and while the slightly cooler air allows us to finish lunch, I realize I can't seem to bring my body temperature down.

I swipe my forehead again. Bone dry. I slide my fingers behind my knees and in my armpits, searching for any sign of perspiration, but I come up empty. After twenty minutes of heavy breathing and fighting off dizziness, I declare to Brita that our romantic picnic in the outdoors must be short lived. "I don't know what to do, babe. I just can't cool down," I say, amidst heavy breathing and continued amazement at my dry skin.

"Let's get out of here. You're definitely overheated."

As we get in the car, blast the A/C, and start driving down the hill, I frantically shake our water bottles, searching for any remaining drops. But there's nothing there. I feel like a cartoon character whose heat builds up so much that his head turns bright red before steam comes screeching out of his ears.

"Stop at the botanical garden, there's a water fountain there!" I yell.

Brita jumps out and nearly plows through some kids, who are standing there like bowling pins, on her sprint to the fountain. Within a minute, she's back at the car. She gasps as she sees me cowering in the passenger seat, fighting to stay conscious. She hands me two full liters of water.

Without thinking, I dump both bottles over my head, effectively drenching the front seat and dashboard. I'm slightly revived thanks to this car seat bath, but don't feel like I'm finished. "More... please. Can you get more?" I whisper.

By the time we're finished, I've dumped six liters of water all over myself, and drunk two more. Strangers in the parking lot are looking at me like I'm fresh out of the nuthouse: sitting soaking wet in the car, with my eyes closed and a massive, ear-to-ear smile as I've finally started to cool down.

As I start to feel more normal, I recognize that this must be yet another indication of how unfamiliar and sensitive my body has become. Of all the things they explained to me in the hospital before I left, there was little mention of the lack of body temperature control that comes with spinal cord injuries. I remember all of the nights in rehab, bundled under four thick blankets, never quite sure of why I felt so cold. Now, it all makes sense. It turns out that my injury occurred above the part of my spinal cord and nervous system that control the autonomic ability to sweat, which aids in effectively cooling down the body when its temperature rises.

Sitting in the hot sun, without the ability to perspire and release heat and moisture was like fastening the lid on a pot and cranking up the flame on a stovetop. No wonder I felt like I was going to pass out or explode.

As we drive back into town, I wonder what a life without sweating will be like. My laundry needs will be reduced for sure, and maybe I won't have to worry so much about what I smell like after I exercise, but being outdoors and doing so much of what I enjoy will take an entirely different form.

Brita catches on to my quiet contemplation and rests a gentle hand on my leg. "It will get better, sweetie. Don't worry," she says.

10.

Wiggle, Wiggle Little Toe

I slowly open my eyes and see the gentle winter sun shining in through the window. I'm groggy and tired from a poor night's sleep, which has become an all-too-common occurrence. For the last eight years, I've been able to remember my dreams when I first wake up, and my dreams have been especially vivid in the six months since my injury. Now I think of the images I saw last night: *A college campus... I'm unclear who the people are around me or where I am, but it feels familiar... I'm pushing an empty wheelchair as I make my way down a hallway... I try to walk faster, but I can't seem to speed up... I carry the empty wheelchair down a flight of stairs and continue to push it as I walk...*

Much like every other morning, last night's dream has me walking and on my feet. It's not always easy, and it often doesn't even feel completely natural, but I'm always on my feet, no matter what. I think back to yesterday's events and how they could have contributed to my dreams, and suddenly all the details come flooding back to me.

***

It was New Year's Day, and my parents suggested to Brita and me that we all make a day trip to Sonoma and the surrounding wine country to get out of the house and change our scenery. It would be good for all of us to break the routine of medications, injections, relentless exercise, and post-spinal cord injury life for a few hours.

So we went through my morning routine and headed out. Just minutes before we arrived in Sonoma, I felt something quickly making its way through my bowels. I had gotten my morning toilet routine down to a rather consistent pattern—a welcome change from the adult diapers I was wearing only a couple of months before—and hadn't experienced any accidents since my days in the hospital. But this morning I had used a different suppository to help me with the process, and something must have gone wrong. Within two minutes of noticing that my digestive system wanted to go rogue and not listen to my brain desperately telling it to hold fire, all hell broke loose.

There I was, a thirty-one-year-old man, sitting in the car and shitting my pants.

What ensued was the most humiliating hour of my life: relentless tears; boundless frustration; and anger at a universe that allowed this to happen, that showed me just how ugly and defeating this injury was, and reminded me that I did not yet know the limit of just how bad things could be. I was embarrassed to ask Brita to step out of the car so my parents could wipe and clean my bottom, like a newborn. If I was no better than a two-month-old baby, I thought to myself, then how the hell was I ever going to take a step, let alone stand on my own two feet?

"It's okay, sweetie, it's totally okay, don't worry," Brita repeated as I continuously apologized to her, unable to hide my shame through the flood of tears.

After we aborted our day trip and returned home, I spent the rest of the afternoon furious, disgusted, and terrified. I wanted so badly to go back to my old life, to escape this living nightmare, to hold Ctrl+Alt+Delete until everything rebooted and I could wake up without the overwhelming challenges of a spinal cord injury.

But a voice inside me responded to the fear and sadness, and reminded me that it hadn't even been six months. Was I already crumbling and preparing to call it quits? I couldn't lose sight of the guy in the hospital who said he wasn't going to stop working hard until he reached his goal. I had to be the resilient and determined fighter who was ready to take on the entire medical establishment, to prove them wrong about everything they said about limited expectations for recovery.

***

It's only been a couple of weeks since my hospital bed was replaced with the well-worn double bed from my old room in my parents' house, and I love that Brita can now sleep next to me instead of curling up on the couch, as she did for the previous months. I see she's still in a deep slumber now, so I lie still and listen to my mom shuffling around in the kitchen, as she waits for my dad to come in and begin his daily coffee-brewing ritual. My mom has never needed much sleep, always functioning on four hours a night without a problem, but it seems like these days, the morning caffeine jolt is a bit more essential than it's ever been.

It's not a surprise that these last six months have been tragically difficult for my parents. My dad, always the more reserved and introverted of the two, has quietly shouldered the burden of my many physical and personal care needs: driving me to and from appointments and treatments, helping me transfer to and from the wheelchair, and dealing with my daily hygiene rituals, among many other things. Despite his quiet nature, he hasn't been without his own challenges, including dealing with anxiety and panic attacks, which have twice led to visits to the hospital.

My mom, who wears her emotions on her sleeve, has reached a level of stress and worry even I didn't know was possible. Upon notification of my discharge from the hospital, she had to scramble to deal with her upcoming schedule of teaching and administrative responsibilities at UC Berkeley. She somehow figured out how to make it all work, thanks to the understanding of the university, and is now spending nearly every waking second helping me, or worrying about me, in one way or another. That said, she will have to go back to work soon, and her looming responsibilities are building stress as she simultaneously mentally prepares for her transition while agonizing over how she will continue to care for me.

As such, I think the last thing on her mind is that today is her birthday.

I reach gently over Brita and grasp the far side of the bed so I can face the window and peek outside into the courtyard. One of our neighbors, a blind woman with a seeing-eye dog, walks past the flowers and succulents that glisten from the overnight drizzle. I decide to go through my usual visualization exercises: flex my feet, bend my knee, rotate my legs in and out. Although I don't get any movement in my lower body when I do these exercises, I've stubbornly and consistently kept at them. The reason everyone—from the nurses in the ICU to my spine surgeon to the acupuncturists—has emphasized the importance of visualization is the belief that there is enormous value in sending a signal from the brain to the lower body. The thought is that by thinking and trying to move those limbs, one can possibly repair the neural pathways and reestablish that damaged connection.

I feel a slight squirming down by my feet and assume that Zara, the family cat, has somehow snuck into bed with us. I glance down at the covers, but she's not there. I grab my side of the bed and roll myself to the other side, then stretch my arms over my head and continue my exercises. I feel the squirming again. Is Brita kicking me under the covers in her sleep? I glance back at her and see that she's lying as still as a corpse, and there's no movement by my feet.

I lie still, now wondering if a mouse or furry critter that set up camp in our tidy apartment has chosen this morning as the chance to gnaw at our ankles. I know how much Brita despises rodents and any "scurrying furry thing," as she describes it, so I start brainstorming how exactly we'll trap the critter. Comical images of my dad chasing after a mouse and Brita and my mom sprinting out of the apartment while I lie helplessly in bed run through my head.

I dig my elbows into the mattress to push myself up to sitting so I can further investigate, but I see nothing at the foot of the bed. The movement has stopped, and I'm nervous about what I'll see under the covers, so I wait. I go back to my visualization exercises and notice that something feels different in my feet, as if something is happening that is not just one of my random spasms or reflexes. A few seconds later, I see a tiny movement in the blankets around my feet, and it definitely doesn't feel like a scurrying animal.

I throw off the covers to get a better view. No cat, no mouse, no critter. Brita will be relieved. I stare at my right foot and see that my pinky toe is slowly dancing in and out. It must be a random movement or a weird spasm I've never had, so I stop my exercise and do nothing.

Pinky toe doesn't move. I start the exercises back up, and there it goes, immediately responding to the signal I'm sending.

This *can't* be right. It's been months and months of having my legs and feet dangle lifelessly as I've dragged and lifted and bumped and dropped them from place to place in this strange new world of life post-spinal cord injury. I try to move it again, this time to confirm if what I've been seeing could actually be real.

"Wiggle little toe, wiggle," I command.

"Wiggle, wiggle," it responds, as it dances back and forth, proving to me that for the first time in almost six months, I have regained motor control of a part of my lower body. I'm still not able to fully comprehend what's happening, so I do it again and again and again. Pinky toe keeps wiggling back at me.

"Baaabe." I nudge Brita gently.

"Mmm… so sleepy…"

Wiggle, wiggle, wiggle. Pinky toe is going crazy. "Babe, I need you to see this and tell me I'm not insane."

She yawns, opens her eyes and slowly sits up.

"Look at my toe. Just look at it," I say, pointing down at my foot.

"It's moving… Wait, it's moving! What??!! Are you moving it?"

"Yes, I think so!"

We both stare incredulously at my right foot as I keep sending the signal from my brain to move the toe, and it keeps responding.

It's time for another opinion for validation, so I yell out to the kitchen. "Mom! Come in here! You have to see this!"

Of course, she immediately thinks something awful has happened as she rushes into the room, expecting a disaster. "What? What's wrong? What happened?"

I curse myself for alarming her like this, but can't hold back my excitement. "Look! Look at my foot!"

"Wiggle... wiggle, wiggle," says my pinky toe.

My mom's expression is a beautiful mixture of shock, disbelief, and unfettered joy. "Are... are *you* doing that?"

"Yup!" I wiggle my toe relentlessly, like a lion tamer whipping its subject into action.

It's difficult to describe the feeling of regaining control over a part of my body I had been told would remain disconnected from my brain, so I try to soak it all in. It's as though a dam that was holding back a wall of water suddenly had a hole poked through, and there's now a flow of water shooting through to the other side. Suddenly, a fear hits me. What if this is temporary? What if the control over my toe is just a momentary neurological phenomenon that will fade away? What if the hole in the dam wall fills back up? If it's only going to last a few minutes, then everyone better see it now.

My mom beats me to the punch and yells for my dad. "Shahin! Shahin, where are you? Come here, come here, come here!"

My dad lumbers in cautiously, not nearly as frantically as my mom's entrance.

"Look at it! He's wiggling it! He's wiggling his toe! He's doing it all himself!" My mom is practically screaming.

"Oh my god..." My father's reaction, as I expected, is muted on the outside, but I know he's just as excited. "You're really doing that?" He finally looks at my face after a minute of staring at my foot.

"Yes I am! Check it out. I can stop moving it, nothing happens, and then I start it up again. I'm totally doing it myself." I get a little cocky, but

I convince myself that it's okay, that once the wiggling stops and I'm jolted back to reality, I won't regret my previous swagger.

Brita jumps out of bed and grabs her phone to capture it on video.

The show goes on for another few minutes before my mom, overcome with emotion, starts calling various family members to tell them the good news. While she's pacing back and forth, spending more time discussing a pinky toe than I ever imagined possible, Brita is jumping up and down as my dad and I keep testing the wiggling, ensuring that it's not temporary.

It's only one pinky toe, on only one foot, and I know it's still a very long way to go before I can move my legs around like I want to, but fresh hope has arisen for the future of my recovery. To go from feeling that controlling any part of my lower body would be the equivalent of bending a spoon with my mind to finally seeing a flicker of hope in a tiny pinky toe is an indescribable moment. My brain has reestablished a connection to my lower body, and no one saw it coming, least of all I.

The single most significant moment of my recovery so far has occurred just a day after the most humiliating and denigrating experience of my life. *Why* is a question I've asked myself countless times since this injury, and while I've never found answers to my why questions, I can't help but ask again now: Why did I have to go through the horror of yesterday, of feeling as helpless as an infant, to then experience the joy of this breakthrough? There must be some supernatural meaning to this, some explanation to which a higher power holds the secret.

Once again, I can't find the answers to my questions, but what I do know is that the fire that fuels my recovery was just doused with gasoline. My conviction to commit myself fully to my recovery, to stay on my path of complete dedication and diligence, has been reconfirmed. The desire to reach my ultimate goal of getting back on my feet has reentered the realm of reality. If it means I have to wiggle this toe 100,000 times until it leads me to control another toe, then so be it. None of that is too daunting anymore. I've made the connection; now it's just a matter of strengthening it.

My mom hangs up the phone and comes in to hug me. "I'm so happy, Arash jaan. This is the best birthday gift I could ever ask for."

"I love you, Mom. I never would have known how to shop for this gift," I say with a snicker, before I hug her tightly, and a shared flow of tears commences between the two of us.

11.

Death, Rebirth, and Recovery

I'm sitting in the bright, airy office of Dr. Dale Hull, admiring the view of the snow-covered foothills that lead to the world-famous ski slopes and towering peaks of Alta and Snowbird, just minutes from the quiet suburb of Salt Lake City, Utah.

"The previous me died when I had my accident," he says as he fixes his gaze upon me. "That guy I knew, the old me, was a nice guy and I really liked him. He was fun and charming and easygoing but he's gone. He left the day I broke my neck on that trampoline."

I've come here to spend a few days at Neuroworx, the nonprofit neurological rehabilitation center Dr. Dale cofounded along with the physical therapist who helped him following his own spinal cord injury in 1999. I learned of Neuroworx from a friend back home, and the moment I read about Dr. Dale's story and got a sense of the comprehensive and progressive approach to recovery employed by the Neuroworx team, I knew I had to make a trip out here to learn more. Since getting on a plane was less than ideal in my vulnerable state, my parents decided we could make a road trip out of this. They packed up the old Subaru, and the three of us made the late-winter drive through the mountains of California and across the vast, empty, and seemingly endless expanse of Nevada to end up here in Utah.

Stepping foot into this place a couple days ago immediately renewed my hope and motivation for my personal improvement. People of various abilities are all welcomed with open arms and friendly smiles, and by a capable staff of neurologically specialized physical therapists, physical therapy assistants, interns, and students from the nearby University of Utah. Although my personal insurance stopped giving me any kind of therapy a few weeks after I was released from the hospital, those who have better health-care plans and continued opportunities for physical therapy can apply their insurance benefits to Neuroworx. Additionally, because it is a nonprofit that raises funds for much of its operational costs, Neuroworx charges minimal rates to people such as me who have to pay from their own pocket, which has made this entire trip possible.

Dr. Dale greeted me the day we arrived and gave me a tour of their incredible facility, all the while leaning on walls and doors near him because he had misplaced his cane. For me, the simple fact of seeing someone with a spinal cord injury walking around on his own two feet was remarkable in itself. It's hard to describe how much inspiration and admiration I felt from seeing him pick up one leg and step it in front of the other with relative ease. It took Dr. Dale over three years of full-time effort and recovery to go from facing the all-too-familiar negative prognosis of his injury to getting back on his feet and running a quarter mile as an official torch bearer for the 2002 Salt Lake City Winter Olympics.

He has just finished telling me the story of the Olympics when he returns to a more somber tone: "That first year after my injury was really hard, as I think it is for most people. Encountering an entirely different body, dealing with all the complications that come with reduced mobility and using a wheelchair, managing incontinence, and figuring out how this new body functions are things none of us are prepared for. I mean, I was a practicing physician, and I didn't work with neurological matters, but I knew enough about spinal cord injury and its basic effects. Yet none of that prepared me for what it would *actually* be like."

"That's what I think about all the time: the struggle to cope with this multitude of factors coming at me from all different directions," I reply. "It was especially challenging at the beginning, and while it's gotten better, it's still so difficult."

"And you'll continue to figure things out, but there will always be so many things you have to do differently than most people. And that's what people will never understand; it's not just the wheelchair and the inability to walk, it's all the invisible stuff—all the trips to the bathroom, the weak hands, the struggles with everyday tasks that others take for granted."

"Exactly. I wrote a blog post about this using the analogy of being on a battlefield and facing your enemy straight ahead, and just as you're starting to fight, there's an army coming at you from one side, then the other, then behind, then above. And the next thing you know, you're surrounded on all sides and can't figure out where to focus your efforts. It becomes overwhelming very quickly. Kind of a living nightmare." I laugh sarcastically.

He chuckles. "I like that explanation."

"But was there a point where things finally got easier for you?"

He exhales slowly before he responds. His demeanor is calm yet not without intensity, and I can see him reliving some of his pain. "Well, that's what I was starting to tell you earlier when I was talking about the death of the old me." He settles into his chair and continues. "You know, when someone dies, there's obviously a process of mourning. People remember that person; they are saddened by the loss. They look back on memories and share stories and talk about how they will miss that person. And while it's incredibly sad and difficult for those closest to the deceased, eventually there is an effort to move on with their own respective lives. The dead one is never forgotten, yet we know he or she is not coming back, at least not in the same form. I don't want to get too deep into talk of the afterlife and such, if you know what I mean…"

"No, no of course, I hear you. Go ahead."

"I didn't come to this conclusion until years after my spinal cord injury, until a lot of time had passed and I was more accepting of this new and different body, but I eventually decided that to move forward with my life, I had to accept that the old me was gone. I know it may sound morbid to some people, but as long as I kept clinging to that person who lived his life without a spinal cord injury and tried to compare my current life to the previous one, it was difficult to be happy. I was only making it harder for myself."

"I don't think it's morbid at all. I think it's realistic. But… wow… I guess I never thought of it that way until you just said that."

"Well, Arash, it wasn't easy because I loved that guy. Like I was telling you earlier, he was a great person, with a happy life, but once the injury occurred, it changed everything. For so long, while I was working hard to improve my physical condition, I wanted to go back to being the old me. In a sense, the thought of re-covering was based on returning to the old me, with all the physical functions I had before this injury. Once I decided to let that person go, and to work with a new body and consider myself a new person, it helped tremendously. I was able to shed the expectations I had set for myself about returning to who I was, and I was instead able to accept myself as a new person and do everything I could to improve my condition with this new body."

"But wasn't it difficult to let your 'old me' go? I mean, I get what you're saying, but I feel like my memories of myself before my injury, and the things I was able to do then, are some of the biggest motivating factors for me to continue to work hard to regain function. I try to be realistic, and I've made peace with the fact that some physical capabilities will be very difficult to regain, but there are so many things I think about doing, and my desire for doing those fuels me and motivates me so strongly to stay on this path of recovery."

Dr. Dale quickly flashes a wise smile, possibly imparting that he knows exactly how I feel right now, that he remembers being in this same place himself. "I couldn't agree with you more. And I don't want you to change anything that will motivate you. I don't think you should accept what the doctors have told you and just 'live with it'; all I'm saying is that for me, seeing myself as a new me and working to improve my situation weren't mutually exclusive. I got a certain peace and serenity from accepting that the pre-spinal cord injury me was gone and I could still be an incredible, successful, happy person, even if it would be under different circumstances, with completely different capabilities."

My head is spinning from this whopper of an existential perspective that Dr. Dale has handed me. "So, how did you do that? How did you finally let that person go?" I ask timidly.

"I held a wake for myself," he says, his eyes gleaming with sincerity and intense emotion. "I had a little ceremony in which I remembered and recognized that person and everything he had done. I cried and mourned and tried to come to terms with the fact that it was a death of sorts, that he was gone."

"And then?"

"I was more at peace with myself. I kept improving and working hard, and I became Dale post-SCI. This Dale is obviously not the same as the pre-SCI version, but this guy isn't too bad. I'm grateful I can walk, but as you can see, my walk isn't the same. It's a different walk, not as good as it used to be."

"Dr. Dale, your walk blows me away! I'd be through the roof if I could walk like you. It's so inspiring!"

"That's nice of you to say," he says, laughing. "But you're on the right path already. Keep working hard and doing what you're doing, and you'll figure it out. You've got a great head on your shoulders, and a wonderful family and support network. That's essential for being able to get better after this damn injury."

At that moment, almost perfectly on cue, a couple of people enter the office to greet Dale. "I'll be right back, Arash. I have to talk to these guys for a minute," he says and politely excuses himself and slowly walks out of the room.

As I start to contemplate his words, I'm flooded with questions. Should I be doing the same thing as Dr. Dale? Should I be holding a wake for myself and essentially accepting that the old Arash is gone? Is the old me—the me who climbed mountains and ran races and backpacked and biked all over the world, the me with the insatiable sense of adventure that always fueled me to continue exploring and savoring every second of this precious life—is that me gone forever? Should I be accepting this as a death and mourn for myself and move on?

Suddenly, the bright airy office I'm sitting in feels very lonely and grim. The sunshine streaming in through the windows is piercing and menacing. The mountains in the distance now seem threatening, like reminders of a past life and experiences that will live on only in my personal history, likely not to be felt or relived again. For a few moments, all the hopefulness and optimism I've acquired from my previous days here at Neuroworx are suspended and replaced with a dark cloud of apprehension and doubt. I sit silently, staring out the window and continuing to think about the reality of my own living death, rebirth, and recovery.

I try to relate everything I've seen and learned during these days in Utah to my efforts going forward. So much of what I've seen from Dr. Dale inspires me: his personal recovery; his success in creating a thriving center that provides help to many; and his ability to move past his former life, accept his injury, and embrace his new body with a grace and maturity I'm not sure I embody quite yet. However, despite the resonance of his approach and its inherent logic, holding a wake for myself and saying goodbye to the me of my first thirty years just doesn't feel right. I recognize the significance of Dr. Dale's idea, yet I decide to put it on the backburner for now.

As I do this, the cloud of doubt and despair starts to drift away. Taking a break from my intense rehab routine to drive to Utah and learn from everyone at Neuroworx has been eye opening and motivating. I am grateful for this opportunity and can't believe I questioned the value of this trip, even for a moment. If I learn nothing more during my remaining days here—which I doubt will be the case—the conversation I just shared with Dr. Dale has validated my entire trip.

I look up to see Dr. Dale slowly walking back into his office, and I feel an invigorating rush of energy flow through me. I am inspired and I know there is potential for a stronger and more improved body. Maybe for the first time, I am truly grateful that I didn't die from that thirty-foot fall onto concrete. I survived, and now I have a chance to remake myself—yet what form that takes and how I will pursue it remain to be seen.

12.

My Prison Sentence

The pedals on the stationary bicycle come to a halt, and I look up at the clock. It's 2 pm, and I've just finished my four-hour exercise and rehab session, the last hour of which was on this specialized bike. I'm still amazed that I can strap my legs and feet into this bike, attach the sticky pads—which connect to cables that plug into this expensive machine—to my thighs and calves, and the electric signals sent from the bike cause my muscles to contract, and in turn, pedal the bike.

This is how I cap off every session here at the specialized spinal cord injury gym that I discovered after my health insurance denied me any additional PT, and my escapades with Valentine and Jana ended. I've been coming here three times a week for almost eight months, with the exception of my brief excursion to Utah a couple months ago. It requires a one-hour drive each way—assuming traffic isn't bad, which is *not* a good assumption these days in the Bay Area. Since I'm still too weak to drive a car or do anything independently, someone has to spend almost an entire working day driving me back and forth, not to mention staying occupied for the entirety of my exercise session. Because of his flexible work schedule, it's usually my father who drives me, but a few loyal friends have also stepped up and taken turns jumping into our aging Subaru (with just the right trunk size to accommodate my wheelchair) and making the trip out to the gym.

I'm still shocked by the fact that in an area of over seven million people, with Silicon Valley and the innovation hub of the world in our backyard, and with UCSF and Stanford (two of the most prestigious research medical centers in the country) and some of the largest biotechnology firms around, there are virtually zero choices for exercise, rehab, and continued care for people with spinal cord injuries and neurological conditions. I have met some people who drive two to three hours each way to access the specialized program and equipment the gym offers. Since it isn't officially run by physical therapists or doctors, the exercise is not covered by any insurance plans, which means all the clients are either paying the extremely high rates out of their pocket, or like me, they have had to raise the funds privately.

I've seen Todd in the gym every time I've been here, but I've never really talked to him. I know he suffered a similar cervical spinal cord injury, but I don't know much beyond the fact that he can now walk on his two feet, with his green walker seemingly glued to his arms at all times. Today I finally have a chance to hear his story. As soon as I'm free of the many straps and buckles that secure me to the bike, Todd waves me over to a quiet corner near the side door of the gym, away from the clients, trainers, and idle family members and caregivers watching from the side.

His first words strike me like a hammer. "You're doing time buddy," he says, as he looks me straight in the eyes, with unwavering intensity and a slight smirk. His melancholy expression could be confused with smugness, but it's something I've seen many times on the faces of others who have dealt with spinal cord injury, and it only insinuates his understanding of my plight.

"I was so pissed when the doctors told me I'd never walk again," he says as he shakes his head. "I just didn't understand how they could say something like that, with so much certainty. Did they do the same with you?"

"Yup. They told me the damage was bad and that the wheelchair was an inevitability for the rest of my life. As soon as I asked about my chances to improve upon leaving the hospital, they shut me down and told me to go on a cruise instead, to try to enjoy life. As if going on a vacation was even within the realm of possibility, with me struggling just to get through each day without hurting or making a mess of myself!"

"You got dealt a bad hand with this injury," he continues, "as bad as it can be, and I can safely assume that whatever you did in your life, you didn't deserve this shit. But now you're stuck with it. You have a prison sentence, and you don't know how long it is. That's maybe the worst part. At least it was for me. Just doing time in your lonely little prison."

"Doing time is right; that's a good metaphor. I wish there was just a little bit more of an attitude of support from the medical establishment, but they really do just leave you out to dry."

"That's what they do. That's why I started coming to this place. I went to a similar rehab gym when I got out of the hospital, and they helped me regain a great deal of function and eventually get back on my feet. But then Jessica and I moved back home and realized nothing of the sort existed outside the hospital. We were ecstatic when we saw that this place had just opened and was providing an option to people like you and me."

"You know what's crazy?" I reply. "My mom first heard about this gym during my last week in the hospital. We started asking the doctors and PTs for their thoughts and suggestions about it, but they wanted nothing to do with it." I feel my frustration mounting, as it always does when I think of my experience with the hospital. "They said I shouldn't worry because I was going to get PT through my health care. But that amounted to one damn hour a week, and it only lasted five weeks! What was I supposed to do then?"

Even as he slouches comfortably, leans back in his chair and his stronger hand fiddles with his crutch, the intensity emanating from his eyes is unquestioned as he responds with restrained calm. "I'm almost nine years in, man. Doing time for nine years, but you know what? I'm *still* getting better. I'm *still* improving, even all these years later. I just don't know how long this prison sentence is for. I've come a long way, don't get me wrong, but I wish there was a release date at some point." He laughs incredulously.

"That's exactly it. I feel like if I was told I had to deal with paralysis for a certain amount of time—say, for two years or three or five, and then it would all get better—I could handle it. I wouldn't be happy about it, but I could do it. Humans are ridiculously adaptable creatures. We've learned this over and over from people who are constantly studying and proving it. But to adapt to this? It's just too hard. I can't imagine it. I won't imagine it. I just don't know how else to think about it or accept this as reality."

He starts to smile. "Don't. Don't accept it. You're fighting the fight. I know you are. I can see it in your eyes. Just don't get impatient. You gotta be in this for the long haul."

"But I'm almost at a year. This is brutal! How long did it take you to start walking, or at least to stop using a wheelchair?"

There's a unique look I've seen a few times only on the faces of those who have suffered severe spinal cord injuries and achieved a significant level of recovery. Each was given a negative prognosis and told a variation of the "you'll never do this, you'll never do that again" statements. They all faced the most dire and defeating odds head on; took up this most impossible of feats, full of unexpected challenges and lacking any guarantees of success; and paved their own path to getting back on their feet. Because the unbearably slow pace of recovery is a persistent and significant obstacle in the way of those who decide to tackle this immense challenge, achieving any level of notable success is almost miraculous, and is recognized as such. These people, these survivors, realize the rarity of their condition and just how fortunate they are to have earned their mobility back, to have fought so hard for something and to have finally achieved this almost unachievable goal. As a result, every time I've talked to someone who has gotten back on his or her feet following a spinal cord injury, and asked this most obvious of questions—"*When* were you finally able to start walking?"—I've seen the same expression I recognize on Todd's face now.

This look conveys the unpredictability of anyone's recovery, the understanding that no two spinal cord injuries are even close to being the same. The approaches and methods one person uses to regain function may not apply to anyone else out there, because it's such a complex injury and recovery involves so many factors beyond just how badly someone broke his or her spine. I think of this look like a secret handshake or an unspoken code that's so subtle it would go unnoticed by anyone who hasn't been through this experience, but it's unmistakably plastered all over Todd's face as soon as he hears my question.

Yet his answer deftly ignores any element of time line. "It was a battle. I can tell you that much. It never really got easier, but I just had to keep fighting. I was determined to walk, I just knew I could get there. And let me tell you, I had to work my ass off, but I got there."

I'm sure he is treading carefully so as not to give me any false hope or unsupported optimism, yet he recognizes that he has the power to enable me, to fuel me, to stay on my own respective path to recovery. "That's great and it's so incredible to see you here all the time, walking around and working out standing up," I say. "It's inspiring to me beyond what you may know. But seriously, how long did you use the wheelchair? I mean, now I only see you with the walker."

He sighs, apparently recognizing he can't escape my questioning, and gives in. "I didn't start walking with the walker until three years after the accident. And then it took me another year to get to the point where I could use the walker full time. It was slow, really slow... I know you've heard it before, but I'm not going to sugarcoat it and say that anything happened fast for me." He glances out the window for a moment, and I can sense that he might be reliving the emotional complexity of his experience.

"For the longest time," he continues, "even though I was walking with support, Jessica would have to bring the wheelchair wherever we went because I couldn't trust my legs. I'd suddenly get tired and literally couldn't go any further. She'd rush to the car, grab the chair, and save me from falling on my ass. It took years for us not to have to bring the wheelchair with us as backup. More than once, I was stuck in a restaurant after a good meal and a couple of beers because I couldn't get up and walk back to the car. It's a strange scene to see a guy walk in on his own, and then see his wife rush out to grab a chair and wheel him out."

"Seriously?"

"Yeah, no joke. Even these days, I have to stop and take a rest after I walk a few steps. It doesn't take me long to recharge, but I still have to stop, find anything to sit or lean on, wait a few minutes, and then continue walking. I've become a master at being able to rest on something wherever I go," he snickers.

I, too, chuckle at his description. Yet I can't help but feel a rushing sense of envy at his situation. Finding a place to lean and sit seems like a comically easy challenge to overcome compared with my present struggle. I can't even stand up and support my own body weight. My mind starts to wander, and I think of all of the hard work I've been through for the last year and how far I still must go to get to the level where sitting and leaning on something is my primary challenge of mobility.

I start to do exactly what I know not to do: I compare my own situation with Todd's. It took him four years to get rid of his wheelchair? That's an eternity! I'm barely at a year, and I'm losing a small piece of my mind everyday; how can I make it to four years? And that's assuming I can do it as fast as he did. This, it occurs to me, is likely why Todd didn't want to talk about time lines. He knew I would go down this path and he wanted to protect me. And in fact, here I am—getting frustrated and sad about my lack of progress, because I might not be on the same time line as Todd, who is living, breathing, standing, *walking* proof of recovery from a spinal cord injury. Then, just as I start to feel resentment toward him for his hard-fought success, I snap myself out of it and tune back into him mid sentence.

"—so that's what I kept telling myself throughout the whole process," he continues. "I was so pissed off at the doctors and I wanted to prove them wrong so badly that I figured it was worth everything I had to commit myself full time to recovery."

"Well, good thing you did," I reply solemnly. My eyes start to drift off again, but this time Todd reels me back in.

"Look, I know the one-year mark scares you, and it feels like an eternity, but you have to believe me, it's going to get better. The first year is really tough, I can't deny that, but don't let these time lines bother you too much. Just stay on your path and keep working as hard as you are, and you'll get better."

"But you know what they all say. It's always, 'what you have after a year is what you're going to have for the rest of your life.'" I try to prevent myself from looking down at the floor as I repeat the dreaded words that have been spewed at me so often by seemingly all-knowing medical professionals. If there is one consistent thing that the doctors and physical therapists cling to, it's this notion that healing from this injury stops no more than two years after the injury, and as much as I've tried to forget this silly statement, it always comes back to haunt me.

"Complete and utter bullshit," Todd replies slowly and vehemently as he shakes his head. "Those bastards are always telling people that, and it gets me so angry. What did I just tell you? I didn't start walking till way after two years! I'm still changing, still improving. I had new developments just a couple months ago, so where's the explanation for that?"

We both calm down a little, and he looks back at me and completes his thought. "You stare that one-year mark right in its face and keep doing your thing, buddy. You're doing great. I see it all the time when you're here. You'll get through that prison sentence, after all."

"Thanks, Todd. I really appreciate you talking with me."

"Anytime. I'm happy to talk to you whenever you want."

And with that, I wheel out of the gym and find my father, who's patiently waiting for me. On the way home, I ponder the cosmic injustice of the invisible judge and jury that have bestowed upon me a prison sentence and punishment I surely do not deserve.

13.

A Jedi Master in Maui

Our rental car pulls into a gravel driveway that slopes down toward a modest little wooden cottage, surrounded by a vast plot of lush green grass and rows of banana and palm trees. It's impossible not to feel energized, inspired, motivated, and yet completely relaxed and calm as the birds noisily chirp away and the flowers and tropical plants glisten from the rain that fell just moments before. This is upcountry Maui, the quieter part of the island, away from all the resorts and hotels and most of the island's tourists. We're minutes from one of the best kite surfing beaches in the world; the only thing disrupting the bright skies and tropical showers is the persistent wind, which is not fierce or annoying but warm and invigorating. The view through the trees is of the deep blue of the Pacific Ocean, which provides a gorgeous contrast with the various shades of green that coexist in this idyllic setting.

As Brita parks the car and we navigate the wheelchair through the gravel and up to the front door, I admire the incredible location of this Pilates studio. A beaming, vibrant woman in her late twenties swings the screen door open and greets us. "Hello! You must be Arash. So nice to meet you!" She gives us both emphatic hugs and pulls us inside.

"Um... Alejandra?" I say with a little confusion, trying to match my expectations of Alejandra, with her Chilean roots, and the smiling blonde I see in front of me who seems as American as apple pie.

"Ha-ha, no. I'm Rachel. I work with Alejandra. She's just finishing up with another client and will be with you in a few minutes. We're so happy to meet you and excited to work with you!"

Her infectious energy and warm and genuine demeanor put me at ease and quell my apprehension at the significant decision I've made to fly all the way to Maui for this next step in my recovery.

***

"She's a *jedi*," Grant said when he first told me about Alejandra Monsalve on the phone.

I had met Grant through mutual friends a couple weeks after my injury. He was a lifelong athlete and fellow full-time spinal cord injury "recoverer" who had committed to accomplishing what doctors told him would be impossible. He and I had a lot in common. On a quiet Sunday, I sat in the hospital courtyard and had my first phone conversation with him. His fighting spirit, boundless positive energy, and infectious personality were a welcome contrast from the doom and gloom and calls for acceptance coming from everyone in the hospital. I was fearful of how I would continue my recovery upon getting discharged from rehab, and his response comforted me.

"There is so much love out there brother! You'll see," he said. You've been through a situation that so few can understand, but I can tell you that the world is filled with open arms and people who will surprise you. Tap into that love, my man!"

He prepared me for the decisions I would have to make on my own to carve out my path of recovery and rehabilitation. Insurance hadn't helped him, and it probably wasn't going to help me, so he suggested I start raising money and finding ways to financially support my efforts.

In the months that followed, I kept in sporadic phone contact with Grant. He had an extremely busy schedule that kept him traveling nearly nonstop, so I was happy to have conversations with him and soak in his positive energy whenever I could. I can safely say that without his recommendations, my search for quality therapy and rehabilitation options would have been much more complicated and time consuming, and would have likely led to different results. Grant's earnest suggestions were a godsend, to say the least, but none was as emphatic as his recounting of his experiences with Alejandra during a later conversation, after his return from a trip to work with her.

"She's living out in Maui, quietly doing her thing, but her experience and knowledge are like no other," he told me. "She knows spinal cord injury and understands the complexity of it. All of that, combined with her knowledge of how the body works, is just magical, bro! Definitely pay her a visit if you can make it work."

It took a few months for me to raise the money, and for Brita to arrange the time off work, but finally, almost a year and a half after my injury, we booked a two-week session with Alejandra.

Just days before our departure, I met Grant in person for the first time, over an early morning breakfast before he headed to a promotional event. I had so many questions for him, so many things I wanted to ask him regarding his recovery and his everyday life, but alas our meeting was much too short. As we said goodbye, I thanked him for recommending Alejandra. His face lit up before he gave me a farewell hug. "The lines! You're gonna learn all about the lines. Soak it all in, bro! I'm so stoked for you to get out there and meet her!"

With that echoing in my mind, I got on a plane for the first time since my injury and flew across the Pacific with Brita to see what this was all about.

***

Inside the studio, as Brita and I are admiring the serene views of lush grass and swaying palm trees, a short, firecracker of a woman with a shoulder-length ponytail, assertive eyes, and a muscular stature that most athletes would envy comes out of the back room and greets us.

"Hi, Arash, I'm Alejandra," she says in a thick Chilean accent, which carries the subtle mark of having lived in Hawaii for years. "We have a lot to do and not a lot of time. I'm ready if you are. Let's get right to work, and we can start to talk while we're warming up and I evaluate your body."

After the ineptitude of the home-care therapists and others I've encountered through my medical insurance—which I'm always quick to admit is largely due to the system in which they operate and to not their personal shortcomings—it is refreshing, to say the least, to meet someone who doesn't want to waste any time and gets right into the action.

I lie on my back on the Cadillac, a large piece of Pilates equipment, with a flat table and a set of metal bars that creates a rectangular frame above and houses the assortment of circular hooks, rings, and bars that attach, slide, and move about the frame. Alejandra attaches different colored springs (reflecting different resistances) to a couple of the hooks looming above me. As she straps the other end of the springs to my

166

ankles and knees, I realize that the Cadillac looks and feels more like a machine for medieval torture than for exercise.

When she asks me—as she does all her clients—to take my shirt off, I feel slightly overexposed in a body that I'm not confident in. However, the warm, humid air invites me to feel at ease and comply with her request, which will allow her to observe my muscles more closely as I move.

"I need to toosh you to get a sense of your strength as I move through your body," she says.

Toosh? I wonder. It's been a while since I've heard someone use this word to refer to a rear end. And how exactly does my toosh relate to any of this?

She continues, "If I'm gonna get anything done, I have to see how your body moves. I have to start poking around to see if those muscles are firing! Are you okay with me tooshing and poking you?"

I realize that in Alejandra's charming and unique accent, *toosh* means touch. The question is more a formality than an actual request for approval, as her hands are already probing my shoulder blades and back muscles. "Are you kidding? Of course you can. I didn't come all the way here to have you just look at me. I've lost all my pride since this accident, so touch wherever you need to touch," I respond with a snicker.

"Okay, good! If I can't toosh you, I can't help you!" she says with a loud cackle.

Alejandra moves gracefully around me, using the help of the springs to move my legs around as she presses her fingers along my thigh and calf muscles, all while she asks questions about my body and recovery. She's mostly silent as I describe my path thus far, the therapies and exercises I've engaged in, the impact they've had on my body, and my unstoppable desire to attain my goal of getting back on my feet. I glance at her face every once in a while and I see a look of such focus and concentration that I assume she hasn't heard a word I've said.

But then she surprises me by interrupting me and asking about my recent therapy. "What kind of pelvic position are you in when you are standing up at your therapy gym?"

"Pelvic position? Um… I have no idea. I can't stand by myself, so the trainers are always blocking out my knees. Once I'm upright, we do different exercises in that position."

Her eyes widen and she starts to shake her head subtly, but enough for me to notice.

"Is that *bad*?" I ask, like a chastised child facing his parents, unaware of his misdeeds.

Her response is free from any fluff or sugarcoating. "Well, Arash, your body is still very disconnected. Your core connection is really weak, so getting you up into standing is probably putting your entire body out of alignment. If you're not able to control your hips and core, then why should you be standing and putting stress on your whole body?"

"I… I guess I never thought of that. And none of my trainers have ever pointed that out. Seems like they want to get everyone standing and out of the wheelchair, so they go to whatever lengths they have to in order to do that, whether it's using straps or belts or all kinds of different things. I've seen some people wrapped up like mummies, with so many straps holding them upright." I chuckle. "I always assumed it was good that people were out of their chairs and standing, but I hadn't thought of the alignment and such."

"Like I said," she replies, with a disapproving sigh, "we got a lot to do in these two weeks you're with me."

As we stretch and move around in her studio, she starts to explain the fundamentals of her method. From what I have encountered thus far, the conventional approach to muscles, ligaments, and tendons is to think of them separately, evaluate the function of each specific part, and then target a muscle (or one or two surrounding muscles) to strengthen, stretch, or stabilize that area to achieve the goal of improving it. For example, the biceps muscle in your arm performs a specific function; namely, to curl your forearm up toward your shoulder. Simple enough. But what about all of those other muscles that connect to your biceps? Or the muscles that connect to the muscles that connect to the biceps? You have to understand all of that to understand why, for instance, some people feel pain in their right shoulder that stems from an aggravation in the left knee.

It's difficult to exactly describe Alejandra's method. She has created her own system of exercise/movement/training/therapy that she calls Neurokinetic Pilates, but it's much more than just Pilates. Alejandra approaches the body differently than others do, but not in an alternative, Eastern medicine, or hippy dippy way. She was trained as a physical therapist, with Western medicine as her background and knowledge base. She places great importance on fascia, the connective tissue that surrounds and connects muscles, nerves, and blood vessels and runs through our entire body and aids in movement, or as in my case, the lack thereof. Fascia, I learn from Alejandra, provides continuity and interrelation between various muscles, so that instead of thinking we have more than six hundred separate muscles throughout the body, it's more like one muscle with six hundred parts that are all interconnected and related.

Now I understand what Grant was referring to when he told me about the lines. By looking at the body and at the potential for movement as an interrelated system, Alejandra examines and works with connected muscles that perform various functions. Her method is based on identifying, correcting, strengthening, and balancing the lines of muscles throughout the body. When it comes to a spinal cord injury and damaged nerves, her belief is that it is possible to achieve movement in those damaged and unresponsive places by bypassing the damaged area and accessing the fascia and muscle lines to create new neurological connections.

When I ask her if the fascia lines have anything to do with acupuncture meridians, she gives me a puzzled look and shrugs her shoulders. "I have no idea, Arash. I don't know anything about acupuncture or Chinese medicine. Everyone knows that fascia exists, I just use it and look at it in a different way."

We spend the remainder of the two hours moving into various positions and performing exercises on the Reformer, Cadillac, Barrel, and other pieces of equipment that are commonly used in Pilates—all under Alejandra's consistently scrutinizing and analytical eyes. She uses pulleys, bands, and cables, and she stretches and yanks me and gets my body into positions it has never been in before. Each exercise consists of multiple simultaneous prompts from her asking me to do what seems nearly impossible. How can I hold my balance in this position without falling over, while still engaging my back muscles, keeping my collarbones open, maintaining my chest in toward my ribs, breathing with my diaphragm, and trying to suck my belly in... *all* at the same time?

The movements are completely unique compared with anything I've done thus far; they require my full attention and concentration, and simultaneously exhaust me. By the end of the session, I'm undoubtedly able to feel energy, engagement, and sensation in parts of my abdominals and core that I haven't felt since my injury. I'm mentally drained from all the focus and energy I've expunged trying to connect to these seemingly dormant parts of my body, yet as we're driving back to the main road and hearing the crunching underneath the tires, my brain is spinning with the possibilities of everything Alejandra has just explained to me. As much as I generally avoid hyperbolizing any experience and want to tame my expectations, I can't help but admit to myself that what I just went through was eye opening, if not a complete revolution of thought.

"So what did you think, sweetie?" Brita asks. She was there the whole time, silently observing everything with her keen eyes that don't miss a thing. I know she must have her own conclusions about what took place, but she's likely trying to make sense of the look of simultaneous wonder, confusion, and excitement on my face.

"My mind is blown."

***

It's the fifth day of working with Alejandra and my body has slowly become accustomed to the challenge of the exercises she puts me through. We have been working all week on trying to establish some movement and contractions in my abdominal muscles. Since my injury, the upper third of my body (everything above my sternum) has steadily improved and gotten stronger, but everything below has remained floppy and dormant. I can't deny that my ego has been affected by seeing my six-pack abs replaced by a rotund Buddha belly—the result of zero control over my stomach muscles—but these last couple of days, it feels like things have been changing.

Alejandra has been targeting my spiral line, a line of fascia that starts at the back of my neck, goes down the middle of my upper back, wraps around my ribs to my external abdominals and hips, and runs down the sides of my legs. She is getting me to engage muscles over which I do have control (my latissimus dorsi) in order to move down that fascial line and get a contraction in muscles over which I don't have control. We've been working on this exercise every day, and so far it has exposed just how weak my abs are. As I sit with my feet off the end of the Cadillac, I use my arms to pull down on a bar above me that is resisted with springs from above. I become a wobbly mess every time she reduces the resistance, which gives me less support and nearly causes me to go tumbling off the table.

Today, she tries something new. She places her hands on the sides of my hips and reminds me to keep my gaze straight. "Look out at the ocean, Arash. Keep your eyes focused on that and don't look down."

I do my best to abide by her commands as I stare at the blue water in the distance. I begin to space out and wonder how warm and inviting the ocean must feel right now, how soft the wet sand would feel under my feet and between my toes if I were strutting out of the water. As I follow my imagination into a happy fantasy, I'm interrupted by Alejandra's exclamation. "There! That's it! You got it! Keep sitting tall and think about tightening your core!"

After nearly eighteen months of having no abdominal control, my stomach is quivering and shaking. A new neurological connection has been forged! It doesn't feel like it used to when I suck in my belly and tighten my abs, but there's no question that this is a huge breakthrough. I pull down with my arms and sit up tall, and breathe and concentrate, and do everything I can to keep this going. After a few minutes of exploring this new neural pathway and trying to implant the feeling into my muscles and memory, our time is up. I lie back in simultaneous relief and exhilaration.

"Nice work today, Arash! I'm so happy we were able to make that connection. You worked really hard this week. Enjoy the weekend. On Monday, when you come back, we are gonna get right back to it and strengthen, strengthen, strengthen!"

***

It's my last morning in Maui, and I'm headed back to the studio for my final session with Alejandra before flying out tonight. Brita flew home a few days ago to get back to work, so my parents have been with me the last few days. It's their first taste of Hawaii after many years of living in California. I'm happy that they, too, have met Alejandra and seen her method.

Over dinner last night, we all recapped how incredibly rewarding this short but significant time has been for my recovery. I feel like, in nine days with Alejandra, I've made more noticeable improvements than I have in the last year. I've gotten a better understanding of the fascia lines and how Alejandra uses them to establish new neurological connections. We've spent every day so far working on that same spiral line connection we first established last week, and my connection to my core and abs has improved every day. I still don't have automatic or conscious control over my stomach muscles, but I've learned that by pulling my arms down toward my hips and trying to cinch my ribs together, I can get a decent contraction of my abs. That initial connection I had to fight so hard to obtain the other day has become more predictable, more repeatable.

At night, I've been reading as much as I can online about fascia, muscle connectivity, and how nerves are integrated into our musculoskeletal system. I assumed that somewhere on the world wide web there would be journal articles that empirically explained what Alejandra so confidently accomplished with me, but I haven't found anything yet. I've searched and searched for information on fascia, establishing neurological connections, and spinal cord injury, but nothing has come up. It seems that the interconnectedness of our muscles and fascia is a relatively new idea (i.e., from the last ten to fifteen years). From what I've found thus far, it's used by the most progressive and innovative exercise professionals and body workers (especially massage therapists specializing in Rolfing). Once again, I'm stuck with the sinking feeling that the paradigm under which doctors and the medical establishment operate to treat spinal cord injury and recovery is outdated and lacking innovation or creative ideas.

I'm already contemplating how I can help spread Alejandra's method to more people when we pull into the gravel driveway and I snap back into reality for my final session with her.

"I was paralyzed and had to use a wheelchair for almost a year," Alejandra tells me as she finishes the rapid-fire stretching and warm-up sequence we've been doing every day. "I didn't have a spinal cord injury—I want to be really clear so I don't mislead you. I fell from a ladder and had a spinal compression in my neck, so it wasn't nearly as bad as your injury, but I know what paralysis feels like. That's one of the ways that I was able to create my method, just by figuring out what I had to do to improve my own body after my injury. Then I figured out how I could apply those ideas to others."

"Wow. I had no idea. And did that experience also help you build your training for Julia and the other Olympic athletes you train?" I ask, referring to Julia Mancuso, the most decorated American female skier, who has won six Olympic medals, trains regularly with Alejandra, and cites her as one of the biggest factors in her success.

"Absolutely! Arash, to get movement in a body that can't move is so exciting! It's such a challenge! But when it happens, I feel so happy. So, to go from that to working with Julia, who is so strong and knows her body so well, is almost easy for me!"

"Didn't you say Julia invited you to go to the Sochi Olympics with her? Are you excited about going to Russia?"

"I'm happy she invited me and that I can help her, but I hate the cold, Arash!" She cackles loudly. "That's why I moved to Maui! I never wanna be cold. Whenever I am near the snow, I am freezing and uncomfortable the entire time!"

Our last session is much like the previous ones, with me pouring all the energy and effort I have into concentration on a multitude of different body parts at once, and trying to widen this new neurological pathway Alejandra has uncovered. I'm still in a state of pleasant disbelief at the fact that my abs are finally waking up.

As we finish our final exercises and get ready to say goodbye, Alejandra gives me specific instructions on how to continue my exercises at home. "Tell your trainers to always pay attention to your pelvic position and to maintain good alignment," she says.

I nod approvingly, even though I'm already fretting about the transition to working with anyone but her. In her time with me, she has gained a better understanding of my body than anyone else has thus far, and I don't know if or how I can explain her suggestions to my usual trainers. "Thank you so much for everything. I have to come back again soon. It wasn't easy to make this trip happen, but this experience has really opened my eyes. You've renewed my hope and faith in my ability to heal and improve."

"Arash, you know me a little now and understand that I never tell people anything just to give them hope or make them happy, so I'm not gonna do that with you. Nobody knows how your body's gonna heal, nobody knows how soon you're gonna get better. All you can do is work hard. I've seen it in you so far and you want it so bad, so just keep going, keep fighting, and don't listen to anyone but yourself. Whenever you are satisfied or think you're working hard enough, just ask yourself if you can push yourself more and work even harder. That's how you're gonna get better."

"You don't need to worry about that, Alejandra. I never think I'm working hard enough. I always feel like I could be doing more, and it's so refreshing to hear you say I should work harder. I like that better than everyone telling me to take it easy and accept my current body. I'm gonna come back here. I have to."

"You're welcome anytime. I hope to see you soon."

With that, I go out into the gravel driveway and load up into the rental car. I reflect on everything I've discovered about my injury, my body, and my recovery as we coast along the winding highway to the Maui airport.

14.

Southwest Road Trip

It's dark, extremely dark, as we drive east on highway 190 and enter the vast desert of Death Valley, an expansive area larger than New Hampshire. The sun dipped below the parched Eastern Sierra Mountains behind us only minutes ago, yet here under the tranquil night sky, which is filling with more stars by the minute, it feels like it's the middle of the night. The odometer sails up to eighty miles an hour as the curves give way to a straight path knifing through the treeless landscape, which is nursing waist-high mesquite trees and tumbleweeds. We've been in the car for almost eight hours, happily trading the traffic and tailgaters of the Bay Area for the chance to drive for nearly twenty minutes without seeing another car.

"I think we should power through to Furnace Creek and the main campground there," I tell Brita, trying to ignore the searing pain in my low back and butt, a daily consequence of my injury that has become an all-too-normal part of my everyday existence. I knew before we left that a ten-day road trip, covering twelve hundred miles and four national parks across four states, would test my pain threshold, so I'm trying to be a good sport and recognize that I can't wave the white flag of surrender and complain about discomfort on the first day. "I know we talked about stopping at the smaller campground coming up, but it's not much further to Furnace Creek."

"Sounds good to me, as long as you're okay sitting for another little bit," she says.

"I've been in pain for almost the whole drive, what's another twenty minutes?" I say with a smile. "It also means one less setup and pack down of the tent." I know that's music to her ears, and it's part of the compromise we made when we planned this trip. I insisted we camp at least a few nights and then reward ourselves with hotel stays toward the end of the trip. She agreed, although I know at this moment, she's not looking forward to setting up a tent, using only a headlight in the pitch black of the desert. "At least we don't have to worry about bears! And I don't think the rattlesnakes want anything to do with us," I joke as I glance over at her.

Brita isn't a camper. It's not that she doesn't love the outdoors; she does. After all, she grew up skiing in the Minnesota winters, a feat few can boast. Her appreciation for nature, travel, and adventure is one of the things that drew me to her when we met. Everything about her seemed *too* right, so I figured something had to be seriously wrong or lacking. When I found out she had not done much camping before, I decided to test her. If she could make it through a weekend with me—sleeping in a tent, climbing off trails, and dealing with my near obsessive compulsiveness in the camp kitchen as I prepared gourmet meals with a two-burner Coleman stove and the Swiss army knife that was an old-yet-treasured gift from my father—then she was a keeper.

On that Memorial Day weekend trip, almost exactly three years ago, we ventured east of Yosemite and found a remote canyon north of Mono Lake where we could escape the crowds. Every campsite and motel room in a hundred mile radius was packed with families and vacationers celebrating the beginning of the summer season in the mountains, but somehow my research led us to this gem of a campground tucked beneath the Sawtooth peaks and alpine lakes of Tioga Pass. The small fishing shop was closed and there were no signs for the campsites at Lundy Canyon; instead, a burnt-out car, likely from the 1930s, greeted us as we made the tree-covered corner our home for the next few nights.

"So... do you think it's okay that we stay here? Are we allowed?" Brita asked, showing the first sign of concern at coming to this remote location with a guy she had only known for a couple of months.

"I'm sure it's fine. We'll go back to the store later and see if someone is there so we can pay or sign in."

"Okay, that makes sense." She wandered around the site, seemingly unsure of what to do, as unseasonably cold wind blew snow flurries in our faces. Our trip had already faced an unexpected detour the previous day when a freak snowstorm closed the road and blocked our access through Yosemite. We were forced to cook fish tacos while huddled under the open trunk door of the Subaru Forester, and later listened to a band belt out covers of Tom Petty and Bob Seger in the oldest saloon in California, a token from the Gold Rush.

The snow in Lundy Canyon wasn't wet or dense enough to stick to the ground, but it made the setup tricky for me. "I'll pitch the tent and get our mats and bags set up real quick. Just bundle up and stay warm, and then maybe we can go for a walk by the lake before we come back to cook dinner." I was so intent on making our first camping experience enjoyable that I politely refused her repeated offers to help, preferring to piece together the poles and attach the nylon rain fly on my own. After all, this was what I had grown up with; it was my home turf, and I knew it would take longer to explain any desired assistance than to efficiently complete everything on my own. I loved the ability to do all of this independently—to effortlessly blow up our sleeping mats, to reach into the cooler I had meticulously arranged and grab the vegetables for our Indian curry dinner, and to strum my guitar by the campfire and serenade the two of us.

Now, as I bring my focus back to the empty desert road leading to Furnace Creek, I am struck by how much has changed since that Memorial Day weekend in Lundy Canyon. Preparing for this trip was different than for any other trip in my memory. This time, my dad had to gather all the camping gear and organize it into the same plastic boxes he's been using since my childhood camping trips. He had to pack the car for me, patiently abiding by my instructions about where to put everything to make it easier to reach. And while I was able to chop up and prepare half a dozen containers of food to sustain us through the first few days, I couldn't shop for the ingredients or organize the cooler without Brita's help.

After we arrive at the Furnace Creek campground, Brita assembles the tent and listens to my attempts to be instructive without being too bossy. I grit my teeth and try to suppress my frustration at yet another indignity of my injury: I'm unable to be the master of the campsite, unable to relieve her of all the tasks she now has to take on to help me and to help the two of us. As she finishes with the tent and starts to unpack the car, my anger pokes its head out and starts to build. But tonight I won't let it get the best of me. Tonight, the warm air, beauty, and serenity of the desert—a place I love so dearly—will lull me to sleep and remind me that as much as some things have changed in my life, others have not. I'm still able to gaze at the night sky through the roof of the tent and quietly drift off to sleep.

***

It's still late morning, but it's already scorching hot when we park the car at Badwater Basin, the lowest point in the Western hemisphere and one of the more well-traveled tourist sites in Death Valley. Fortunately, national parks, as federal institutions, must abide by the Americans with Disabilities Act (ADA), meaning that all parking lots and main tourist sites must be made wheelchair accessible.

I never used to pay attention to accessibility or stairs or ramps or grab bars or wide bathroom stalls. All I knew was that the blue "handicapped" (a term that is nearly ubiquitous, but that I never use) parking spot, with the little logo of a wheelchair, was a big no-no for me. I suspected a cop would appear out of thin air were I to occupy one of those spaces, even for a few seconds. Now, all I see whenever I go anywhere is accessibility. *Could I go there? How steep is the ramp? Does the elevator work?*

"Is the path down there accessible?" I ask Brita, pointing to the salt flats below. This question has become an all-too-familiar refrain when we are somewhere new. I always wait in the car as Brita jumps out and surveys the pavement and landscape for any sign of stairs, bumps, dirt, or challenging terrain. I love how she skips back to the car, smiling proudly when the news is good and we are able to access a place with the wheelchair.

Now, she affirms that the hard-packed salt path is fine. We get out into the ninety-five degree heat and make our way down the path. On our way, we are passed by throngs of Europeans, mostly French and

Germans, easily identifiable by their clothing and footwear, if not their silent glances as they pass me.

"Wow, the French really are out in full force, aren't they?" Brita chuckles.

"Yeah, I told you, babe, the Europeans love the Southwest. They have nothing like it in Europe, so they flock here. Wait till we get to Bryce Canyon and Zion. It's crazy."

After almost a decade of frequent international travel before my accident, I haven't left the country in more than three years. In fact, my passport expired two years ago, and I've had no reason to renew it because going abroad with my current situation has seemed nearly impossible. As such, this is the highest concentration of non-Americans I've been around. Throughout the day, most of the European tourists avoid all eye contact and don't greet me as they pass us. They remind me of people walking by a homeless person on the street, hoping that person won't bother them. I haven't yet figured out the reason for this lack of interaction, but both Brita and I notice and discuss possible explanations.

"It *has* to be because of the wheelchair. What else could it be?" I grumble.

Brita is always more willing to give people the benefit of the doubt than I am. "Well… no," she says now. "Some of them look like they're deep in conversation and maybe didn't notice."

"Really, babe? C'mon… You know it's because of the chair. They're probably not used to seeing it out in the open like it is here. The U.S. is great that way. I almost never get weird looks from people. But I've heard from friends that it can be really tough in other countries where people aren't used to seeing wheelchair users."

"Maybe they've seen from far away how handsome you are and don't want to get caught staring at you!" she says with a huge grin.

I can't help but smile. I've been silently cursing the wheelchair with every push of my arms as I struggle to get momentum across the arid, crunchy dirt underneath my wheels, but her response calms me down. I love her ability to diffuse my frustration or resentment and turn it into something positive. I start to tear up as I recognize how grateful I am for all she does for me. Despite her weak right arm—recently fractured from a fall on her bike—she gives me a boost with her stronger left arm, as we make our way to the edge of the salt flats. Once we are there, we realize we are alone and cherish the momentary solitude and the magnificent view.

**

In the peak heat of the late afternoon, we decide to make one more stop before heading back to our campsite. As we near Golden Canyon, where we have agreed that Brita will take a short hike without me, I finish telling her about my only previous trip to Death Valley, five years earlier. I went with Laura, my childhood friend and sister-from-another-mother. I was on spring break in the first year of my MBA program, and Laura was taking a much-needed vacation from a busy winter of consulting work. "We ran this canyon in the morning, then did a huge bike ride at lunch, before doing another hike in the afternoon. I'm telling you, we dominated this place!" I tell Brita, sounding more than a tad boastful.

Brita smiles as she listens to me recount the frenetic pace of activities Laura and I undertook. We treated our five days here like a multisport

Olympic training retreat: hiking, biking, running, and exploring our way through the slot canyons, sand dunes, and mountains of this diverse landscape. I'm overcome with an all-too-familiar emotional concoction of reminiscence, frustration, and anxiety at the thought of not being able to do these things I previously did so capably. It was all so easy then; it all came so naturally. I asked my body to move, and it moved. On that trip, I challenged myself tremendously, and my body responded. When I decided to ride my bike for the longest continuous uphill I had ever undertaken—twenty-six miles of climbing, with 5,700 feet of elevation gain—I willed my tired legs to push me to the top. When I finished sprinting through a slot canyon, I was happily surprised I hadn't sprained my ankle on the unstable rocky surface. I took care of my body, and my body took care of me.

Now, every movement is a struggle. If I lean too far forward, I fall out of the wheelchair. If I'm not careful with my weakened wrists (also injured during my fall), I can impair a body part that has become essential for all of my transfers in and out of the wheelchair, and thus for everything I do. Since I'm still not able to take any steps or stand, I live in a consistent daydream in which I am slowly analyzing every movement involved in walking ten paces and trying to replicate it mentally.

Before I get too deep into my fantasy, Brita snaps me back into reality. We arrive at Golden Canyon, and she gets out of the car and leans in through the open window to the driver's seat to kiss me. "Are you sure you don't mind waiting for me to do the hike? I feel bad leaving you here," she says.

"Not at all. This is why we're here. You have to see these places, even if I can't be there with you. At least you can rest assured that I've seen all of them before." This comforts her enough to leave me and push her way through the sweaty and sunburned tourists and charge up the canyon.

***

It's a brisk afternoon in Bryce Canyon National Park, unusual for late May, when the long days and high altitude sunshine typically impart a prolonged warm soak for the many hoodoos. These unique, tower-like geological formations, carved by years of erosion, wind, and water, are unforgettable characteristics of this park and give it a planetary feel unlike anything else.

It snowed on us last night and this morning, at the most inconvenient times. After the desert heat of Death Valley, this sudden change in the weather has caught us off guard. We didn't think that a thirty percent chance of precipitation would mean a solid stream of snowflakes precisely when we would be cooking dinner at the campsite, but that's what we experienced. We assumed one meal in a winter wonderland was sufficient, but we were lucky enough to have another round of the white stuff just as we were boiling hot water for our morning coffee. Brita was in the bathroom when the weather changed, and I felt close to useless as I rolled around on the wet pine needles and mud, trying to throw things into the dry car from my wheelchair. It frustrated me to no end not to be able to take control, as I had done so many times in my life, and to have to rely yet again on someone else to do for me what I couldn't do myself. I mistakenly channeled my frustration toward Brita and complained about the way she was dealing with the situation, instead of recognizing and appreciating her for being so patient and willing in the challenging circumstances.

After breakfast, I sent Brita out to do my favorite hike and assured her that I didn't mind waiting in the lodge. Now, as I lounge in the decades-old leather chair and try to attract as much warmth as possible from the roaring fire across the room, my ears perk up at the sound of the tourists sitting next to me, huddling over their hot chocolates and sorting out how to deal with the inclement weather. I don't understand any Dutch, but I recognize it easily, differentiating it from German or any of the Scandinavian languages. Its sing-songy sentences are familiar to me, not only from the countless young Dutch travelers I've met all over the world, but also from the elderly Dutch couple who housed me when I worked in rural Portugal for weeks at a time in my previous life as a trip leader. My mind starts to wander as I remember living on their farm outside the city of Evora, and their heated yet loving exchanges with each other. I suppose hearing them banter and yell at each other tuned my ears to the sound of the language.

I'm blasted back to reality by a gust of frigid air as a group of middle-aged Americans swing the door open and come huffing and puffing inside. Immediately, I hear them complaining. They complain about how difficult the hike into the canyon was, how cold it was, how unpleasant it was, and how nice it is to be back in the warmth of the lodge. I look up and beg the world, the universe, God, Baby Jesus, or any higher power willing to listen to me to let me trade places with these people, even just for a day.

They don't know how good they have it. They don't realize that even on a frigid spring day, seeing and exploring this incredible park on foot, as it's meant to be seen, is a privilege. If it were up to me, I would spend the entire day outside the lodge, hysterically smiling and grinning, taking in the grandeur and beauty of this place instead of dealing with the challenges of recovering from my injury. I try not to brood as I recognize that I'm unable to do these hikes in the canyon, unable to show this sacred place to the woman I love and share her excitement at seeing it for the first time, but I'm interrupted.

Brita leans down from behind me and presses her cold face against mine. "That was incredible! What an amazing place."

"Believe me, I know…"

"Were you okay waiting for me again? I tried to hike as fast as I could so you wouldn't get bored here."

"You shouldn't have rushed, babe. We're here so you can see these places! I was just curled up by this fire and people watching."

After we head out of the lodge and get back to the car, I insist we make one final stop before we leave the park and head to our next destination. The path from the parking lot to the Bryce Point view area is paved but steep, and Brita struggles to help me push to the top. Some tourists are better than others at dodging me as I navigate my way around. All of them though, it seems, are bewildered at the site of me doing exactly what they are: seeing the view, taking photos, smiling and chatting with my girlfriend. The trend of avoiding eye contact with me continues. Most don't even reply to Brita's friendly greeting as we walk past them; instead, they focus on correctly attaching their smart phones to their selfie sticks.

Back at the car, I prepare for another long drive by sitting back in the wheelchair and trying to straighten my legs in front of me. It's a movement I've become more adept at recently, and while I don't always get a consistent response from my legs, it still feels good to try to get the blood moving a bit. My body doesn't like the cold weather, and my legs feel stiff and unresponsive. Just as I'm getting ready to get back in the car, I look up and see a woman hastily approaching me.

"Oh my gosh! I'm so glad to see you here by the car instead of sitting up in that wind. I was getting worried about you up there!" she says.

I try to muster up a polite response, even though I'm furious and humiliated on the inside. I want to scream at her and ask if I look that fucking helpless. *Did you just see everyone else up there? Do I look that much more fragile and vulnerable than the tourist girl with the high heels and the Hello Kitty purse?*

The best I can do is tame my grimace and nod silently before she walks away.

***

"There it is, check it out. The biggest ditch in the world! No ditch you've ever seen quite compares to this one!" I've used this joke every time I've come to the Grand Canyon. Because it's been a few years since I've been here, it feels satisfying to say it again, despite how lame a joke it is. Thankfully, Brita has always been patient with my quirky and odd sense of humor. I'm grinning proudly as we make our way closer to the edge, as if I had something to do with creating this magnificent spectacle of nature. "It's pretty amazing, isn't it?"

"Wow, it's beautiful. I can't believe how clearly you can see everything, all the way to the other side of the canyon. That's the south rim, then?"

"Yeah. Ninety percent of people who visit the Grand Canyon go to the south rim, so it's kinda nice to be here on the north side, which is so much quieter and has just as nice a view."

Being back at the Grand Canyon is flooding me with more memories of leading family camping trips here for my old job at Backroads, an active travel company with biking and hiking tours all over the country and the world.

There was the time I was cooking dinner for our group of twenty-six people when it started to rain. Within moments, the rain had transformed into a monsoonal down pour. When it finally stopped, I had to fix the awning on the side of the trailer. The awning had been protecting me as I tried to chop vegetables and boil soup, but the weight of the accumulated water caused it to collapse. I had to furiously dump buckets full of water from the stove and food supplies into the small river that had formed in the campsite road, sandwiched between our tents and the heretofore seemingly indestructible 12-cylinder Ford van, which was now threatening to float down into the canyon. When the park ranger came by to check on us that evening, just as I had somehow salvaged the dinner and fed the hungry masses, he told me that it was the heaviest rainfall they'd measured for a one-hour time period. *Ever.* Just my luck, I thought to myself.

I glance back toward the lodge, built beautifully on the edge of the rim, and another memory comes back to me.

On a different trip to this park one year later, a family of five were tormenting all of us trip leaders and most of the other families by consistently complaining about anything and everything. During our second night at the Grand Canyon campground, still three days from the end of the trip and a much-anticipated farewell, my coleaders and I had had enough. We were boiling over with frustration and knew we had to release it. The four of us jumped into the van, rolled up all the windows, and let loose verbally. We yelled, we whined, we cursed, we gossiped.

When we were exhausted by it all, we tumbled out of the van. Too tired to put up a tent for ourselves, we curled up on the tarp and slept side-by-side in our sleeping bags under the stars, acknowledging that somehow even annoying, griping people couldn't match the serene beauty of one of the world's natural wonders.

As we make our way along the paved trail that traverses the rim of the canyon, I point out a tree to Brita and tell her to smell it.

"*Smell* the tree? Why?" she says as she makes a face.

"Trust me. Just stick your nose in the bark and take a whiff," I smile. I'm reminded of all the guests who reacted like Brita when I told them to do the same thing. Inevitably, as soon as one person would smell and summon the others, there would be a circle of humans, large and small, surrounding the Ponderosa pine, with their noses nuzzled into the reddish bark.

"Oh wow, it smells... familiar... What is that?" she says, as she sniffs repeatedly.

"It's cool, isn't it? Most people say the scent is vanilla or butterscotch. I think that's pretty accurate."

Brita keeps telling me how much she loves going to these places with me, having her own personal trip leader who gives her suggestions about where to go and what to do. I'm flattered she feels this way, yet can't help but feel inadequate and upset that I can't do more with her.

I have to tell her which trails to take instead of walking alongside her. I have to look at her photos of the views and combine them with my memories from nearly a decade ago instead of seeing the sights anew. I try to reconcile being the trip leader who can't lead the trip the way he wants, as we leave the Grand Canyon and head to our next destination.

***

Of all of the places I have ever visited, of the thirty-seven countries on six continents I've had the fortune of traveling to, Zion National Park is one of my top three favorites. I always thought it was ironic that I sought to travel to faraway, exotic, and unique places that were different from the world I grew up in, yet one of the places that had the most profound impact on me was right here in the Southwest.

My jaw literally dropped the first time I saw Zion. I was speechless. I was contemplating if what I was seeing could actually be real, and—since it did seem to be quite real—why everyone who had ever been there wasn't shouting from the rooftops about how special and magnificent a place this was. Time after time, I came back to this park, expecting to have finally reached a point of indifference, of shrugging my shoulders and accepting that I'd gotten used to it and wouldn't have the same admiration as on the previous visits. But it never happened. I never tired of this place. I never got bored.

In fact, I think that with each visit, I was able to deepen my appreciation and love for the sloping checkerboard mesas; the massive Navajo sandstone cliffs towering over the valley; and the serene flow of the Virgin River, carving its way through the park, reminding visitors of its historical role as the primary cause of the special geology of this place.

Throughout our trip so far, I've done my best to quell my excitement and undoubted favoritism toward Zion. Brita knows how much I love it, how much I've looked forward to coming back here, how I planned our entire trip with us ending in Zion so we could save the best for last. Although I've tried my best to hide my excitement and give her the opportunity to make up her own mind, I can't hold it in any longer.

We're driving through the mile long tunnel that connects the stunning east side of the park with the unbelievably, indescribably, speechlessly stunning central canyon, surrounded by its legendary sandstone cliffs. This was always my favorite part of leading trips here: driving through the tunnel, the guests unaware of what was about to hit them, and then the silent expressions of awe and wonder as we emerged from the pitch black tunnel into the explosions of color and dramatic scenery in front of us.

Brita's reaction as we exit the tunnel doesn't disappoint me.

"Oh, my, god… Really? This exists? Something like this really exists? I can't believe it. This is incredible!"

I drive well below the twenty mile per hour posted limit, savoring every second, looking for the best pullout for a stop among the sloping switchbacks that wind down into the canyon floor. She doesn't believe me when I insist I'm probably as excited about seeing these views as she is, but it doesn't matter. I'm here now. I'm back in this most sacred of my sacred places. All my frustrations, all my concerns and apprehensions regarding my limitations and struggles, seem irrelevant, if just for a few brief but extraordinary seconds. I roll down the window, crane my reconstructed, titanium-filled neck in as many directions as possible, and feel endlessly grateful for this moment.

15.

How I Came to Be Aquaman

The fog still lingers over the parched hills as I turn the car onto the freeway and into the flow of the few existing cars. The clock on the dashboard says 6:07 am, and I'm pleasantly surprised not only that we got on the road this early but that a Saturday dawn provides a refreshing reprieve from the near-constant traffic that has become the norm on the Bay Area freeways. Although shorter than it used to be, my morning routine still takes almost a full ninety minutes before I can contemplate leaving the house, so it wasn't easy to heed the 4 am wake-up call and crawl out of bed in the dark. Add to that the challenges of squeezing into a brand-new wetsuit and trying to consume enough calories to fuel me for the morning, and it's nearly a miracle that I made it out of the house in time.

Brita hands me a piece of the banana bread she baked the night before, as I juggle the hand controls, the steering wheel, and the supplemental breakfast with my two hands. "It's kinda dry," she says with a grimace. "I could have made it better."

I've become accustomed to hearing her downplay her cooking abilities, so this is no surprise. "I think it's delicious. Better than any granola bar or something I'd get at the store. You know me, I can't usually handle much of a breakfast, but I'm on my fourth piece already. That's saying something, right?"

"I guess, yeah," she says as she rubs her sleepy eyes.

The drive is unusually chatty, considering that neither of us is a morning person and we typically take turns telling the other to be quiet when we first wake up and get moving. As our coffee mugs quickly become empty, the sun starts to peek out. We exit the freeway and wind through the wineries, which have popped up in this area only in the last few years.

"This town used to be pretty quiet. I don't remember fancy wineries or anything when I was a kid and we travelled here for soccer games— just a quiet suburb with a few strip malls and the people working at the famous Livermore Lab. Interesting how times have changed," I say.

Pretty soon the conversation shifts to the present, to what has been in the making for half a year, since I decided to sign up for this long open-water swim. "Do you remember those days in the pool when I had to hold you up the whole time?" Brita asks. "Now look at where you are! You're about to swim more than most people can ever do!"

"Yeah, it's crazy," I mumble as I think back to how this all began…

***

It was my fifth and final week of inpatient rehab at the hospital, when my mom came in the door one afternoon, unable to contain herself. "Arash, you'll never believe this! I heard that when they built this hospital, not even two years ago, they put in a swimming pool with ramps, parallel bars, and everything needed to do water therapy. So I've been asking the nurses and the physical therapists about it for the last few days, and now, finally, the social worker took me over there and showed it to me."

"Wow, that's cool, Mom. Why haven't I heard about this at all? Seems like it could be beneficial to get into the water."

She shook her head, as her expression quickly turned into disgust. "Because these people are unbelievable! The health-care system is a mess! I've been reading about the benefits of being in the water, which is why I was so curious about their pool and why I kept bothering them about it."

"So, what's the story?"

"Well, it's ridiculous. I saw it, and it's a beautiful big space, designed specifically for people with neurological injuries and made to be safe. But it's empty! It's completely empty! There's no water in the pool, and the whole place is collecting dust!" She paced around the room and shook her head vehemently as she ranted. "They told me that when they built the hospital and this new neurological rehab unit, they planned to integrate the pool into their therapy program, but they shut the whole thing down right away. Apparently, the cost of cleaning and maintaining the pool and having the proper staff was too much for them, so they don't even use it! A brand new, state-of-the-art pool, just completely empty. I can't believe it."

"Wow, that's really pathetic," I replied.

She could barely contain her frustration as she looked at me. I could see on her face that she was already mentally crafting the letters of complaint she would send to the hospital.

My first experience in the water occurred during the trip to Salt Lake City, when I met Dr. Dale Hull. Upon evaluating me, the Neuroworx therapists decided it would be worthwhile for me to try aqua therapy in their ninety-three-degree therapy pool. Twice the size of a hot tub and equipped with handles, bars, and installed seats, it was meant to be the ideal pool environment for someone with a compromised neurological system.

As I sat and prepared for the lift to lower me into the pool, I wondered why there were two people in the water waiting for me. *This couldn't be as difficult as working with me on land, with the challenges of gravity and the danger of me crumpling over at any time,* I thought. Yet, the moment I entered the pool, I encountered two very distinct sensations. The first was a tantalizing liberation from gravity and the various pressures that kept my body from being unable to stand up, straighten, and lengthen. The second—and more dominant sensation—was an all-encompassing fear, brought on by the sudden realization that I was much weaker and more helpless than I had thought. Lying on my back in the water, unable to do anything to right myself and resist the weight of my body pulling me under, I started flapping my arms wildly. I fought not to swallow water. I panicked!

At that point, Mike—the burly, barrel-chested physical therapist—effortlessly heaved me upright and pinned my shoulders against the wall. "You all right, bud? Take a couple of breaths. You'll be okay."

Once I realized I could still ingest oxygen and Mike would prevent me from drowning in what was essentially a glorified hot tub, I calmed down and prepared for what would be a different type of exercise than I was used to. We spent the next hour working with foam dumbbells, buoyant straps, kayak paddles, and plastic handles. There were parallel bars in the water that I could lean on to stand up, and a treadmill under my feet that could move under water and challenge me to feel the sensation of attempting to walk in a more weightless environment. Every once in a while, when I would flop backwards under the water or push my limits too far and crumple into the walls, I encountered the same panic and fear I had felt at the beginning. But for the most part, I was overjoyed to move through water without the physical limitations that gravity imposes.

Before I knew it, I was being raised out of the pool on the lift and lowered back onto the all-too-familiar constraints of the wheelchair.

My father looked at me and smiled. "So, how was it?"

"It was amazing. I didn't feel the usual pain and aches of my body, and I could really challenge myself to move farther out of my comfort zone because I wasn't scared of falling. I think I may need to turn into a fish or whale or something."

My dad chuckled as I contemplated inventing some kind of Mad Max, sci-fi, rolling, mobile, chest-high water tank to replace my gravity-stricken wheelchair.

One Sunday afternoon, a few months after that trip to Utah, Brita and I armed ourselves with all the straps, foam noodles, and water toys we could find at the public pool and jumped in. The children watched in confusion as I thrashed around in the water. I wasn't as helpless as that time in Utah, but I clearly lacked any kind of competency. Brita patiently pulled and pushed me around the pool as she tried to get me into a safe position, while dodging the free-flowing limbs of the kindergartners causing mayhem in the shallow end of the pool. The water was only four feet deep, but it felt like an endless sea waiting to consume me, should I succumb to its dangers without the pimpled, apathetic lifeguard jumping in to save the day. Thanks to a friend's suggestion, I had brought a snorkel, so I strapped it on, flopped onto my stomach, and quickly realized that being underwater wasn't as scary when I could breathe comfortably and see through my goggles.

After experimenting with various foam dumbbells and coming up with exercises that challenged every part of my body, I asked Brita to stand me up against the wall to try some balance exercises. It was nearly impossible for her to lock my knees out with her legs, pin my shoulders with her hands, and still try to make sure I wouldn't crumple sideways into the water, but she did her best. We checked off a small accomplishment on our humble list of ways to thumb our noses at the medical insurance companies and show them we could create our own aqua therapy program.

Lastly came my attempt to swim laps, or *a* lap I should say. I threw the snorkel back on, stared menacingly at the other end of the pool, hyperventilated a few times, and went for it. "I am Michael Phelps! I am Michael Phelps! I am..." I chanted to myself, conjuring up my memories of the mer-man-like Olympian as I began the journey down what were the twenty-five longest meters of my life. My upper back, neck, and core were still so weak that I couldn't get my arms out of the water. I splashed and thrashed and did everything I could to lift my arms and take a half-decent stroke, but to little avail.

About three minutes later, I reached the wall on the other side, spit out the water that had accumulated in my snorkel, and panted heavily. "I am the furthest thing from Michael Phelps..." I muttered to myself, begrudgingly accepting how far I was from even the eight-year-old version of myself, who could spend the entire day in the pool at summer camp. "I've got a waaaays to go," I said to Brita.

"Well, it's a start!" she stated without hesitation, her inherent positivity as apparent and contagious as always.

***

Thanksgiving morning, a year and a half later, another local pool was hosting a fundraising event, called Swim Before You Feast, intended to get people off their asses and out into the crisp air so they would feel slightly less guilty and calorie-imbalanced when they stuffed their faces later that day.

Upon jumping into the pool and going through the motions of what had become somewhat of a routine, I was about to reach for the snorkel and put it on, when I stopped in my tracks.

"What's wrong?" Brita asked.

"Nothing's wrong. I'm just... I guess I'm kinda sick of this snorkel. I think I'm gonna to go completely without it today and see how long that lasts."

"That's a good idea. You can always put it back on later if you want."

While my abilities had improved dramatically since those early days in the shallow end with the kindergartners, my previous attempts to swim without a snorkel always consisted of the same number of laps: *one*. For whatever reason, I couldn't muster up the strength or endurance to get myself to the end of the pool and back without gasping for air and feeling downright vanquished.

I don't know if it was excitement about the ensuing feast or the collective fumes of the dozens of roasting turkeys in the surrounding neighborhood penetrating my nostrils, but on this particular day, I decided enough was enough. I left the snorkel in the bag and set off on my adventure.

I swam one lap, and as always, found myself clinging to the wall to catch my breath. I went for another, telling myself that, if anything, I could hang my hat on the fact that I had doubled my usual pathetic distance. Just as I was preparing to put the snorkel back on and admit defeat, I asked myself if I had it in me to do *just one more*. Could I tough it out just one more time and effectively triple my all-time non-snorkel lap total? Damn right I could, and at the end of the third lap, I asked myself the same question. Did I have just one more lap in me? Sure I did. And so I continued for five, six, seven, eight laps, always asking myself if I had just one more in me, and each time, the answer was an unequivocal yes.

By only asking myself for one lap and no more, the task became feasible, driven by my innate stubbornness that I could always have *just one more* in me. After ten laps, I noticed that it was all becoming easier. I wasn't stopping to catch my breath anymore, and the twenty-five meters to the opposite end were going by unexpectedly faster. As always, Brita was sharing the lane with me, swimming at more than double my pace, quietly keeping an eye on me, yet consciously allowing me to work through my struggles.

When the lifeguard told us the fundraiser was over and the pool was closing—translation: *"It's Thanksgiving, you idiots, I want to get the hell out of here, sit on the couch with my family, and watch football"*—I had swum eighteen laps without a snorkel.

"Eighteen, babe! Eighteen! It used to be just one! Now I'm wondering why I didn't try this before. It felt so good!" I yelled to Brita as we bypassed the decrepit locker room and went straight to the car.

"That's great, sweetie! You're so much stronger than you think. I always tell you that."

That night, the wheels were in motion as I scoured the Internet for a swim competition or race. I was getting discouraged at only finding triathlons, but then I came across one race organizer's website with a dozen or so triathlons that also listed one single swim event: the Catfish

Open Water Swim. I scrolled through the event details and found three distances from which to choose: 500 meters, 1.2 miles, or 2.4 miles. It was a no brainer. Without hesitation, I scrolled over the button for the longest distance, pulled out my credit card, and clicked "Register." That morning, I had proudly powered through eighteen laps, or a little over half a mile, in my cozy little neighborhood pool; now I was signing up for almost five times that distance, at a sanctioned event, with hundreds of other swimmers, in open water, and with six months to train.

***

Now, half a year later, at the Catfish Open Water Swim, I watch the other swimmers huddle in the early morning sunshine, stretch their official race swim caps (with a comical catfish printed on the sides) over their heads, and go through their stretching and warm-up routines. We're still in the car, and Brita is practically wrestling with me in the driver's seat, trying to yank the wetsuit up over my waist, pull the zipper up my back, and cinch it tight.

"Ahh! I can't get this up high enough! Why is this so hard?" she says through gritted teeth.

"Probably because I'm useless! I can't kick my legs down through to tighten it and get my body all the way in."

She ignores my self-loathing comment, something she's done tirelessly since the beginning, and continues to struggle with the wetsuit. After a few difficult minutes, she finally zips it up, leans out of the car, and smiles.

As we make our way down to the lake, I try not to notice the looks I see on the faces of the other swimmers, likely wondering if I've mistakenly showed up at the wrong event. I've always hated the way people look at me in the wheelchair—not because there is malice on their part, but because of my own insecurity at presenting myself to the world in this way: two feet lower than everyone else, literally being looked down upon at all times.

Big orange buoys in the water mark the course, and a bird's eye photo of the lake hangs next to the registration desk. A friendly volunteer greets me. "Good morning! You're swimming the 500 meters today, right?" he says, immediately reaching toward a box full of envelopes.

"Um… no. I'm actually doing the 2.4-mile option. We both are." I pull Brita closer to me, hoping my tall, beautiful, athletic girlfriend can somehow counteract my unimposing presence.

"Oh… Okay, great! Let me get your swim cap and other materials." He walks over to a different box and points to the large map. "The 1.2-mile course is basically a big triangle around the buoys, so you guys are going to do the same loop twice and finish on the far side of the beach. Have fun!"

We make our way down to the rocky beach and meet Justin and some other friends.

"Brotha G, you ready for this? I'm so happy we're finally here, doing this!" Justin says. He has been swimming with me once a week as part of our training, and in the short time we've been friends, we have become increasingly close. His energy and enthusiasm for life are unrivalled among anyone I've ever met and contagious, to say the least. Immediately, he tilts me back on the rear wheels of the wheelchair and pushes me carefully, if a bit recklessly, across the gravel and rocks, to within a few feet of the water.

Before we know it, the other swimmers are entering the water and kicking off toward the next buoy. The race start is staggered by age and ability, so I start in the very last group, after the sixty-plus-year-olds. Brita, still nursing a recently broken elbow, has kindly offered to forgo her competitive instincts and swim next to me the entire time. She is doing this partially for moral support, but also to help steer me because I can only breathe out of my right side and am still not strong enough to bob my head out of the water and look ahead at where I need to go. We strap the buoys between my knees and around my waist—without them I'm basically a sinking rock—and then I flop my head into the water and start to swim.

Before long, I'm able to shake off my nervousness and get into my groove. I run through my usual list of reminders for swimming as efficiently as possible, knowing that even on a good day, I struggle with my technique: *Eyes down, elbows high, drag the fingers across the water, exhale long and slow, smooth consistent breaths, hips follow shoulders, don't windmill the arms, aim the hands straight ahead."*

Soon enough, Brita taps me on the shoulder, indicating I've reached the first orange buoy and it's time to turn. I'm pleasantly surprised at the distance I've covered so far. It's a far cry from the first triathlon I did, when even with a completely able body, I swam so crookedly and off track that the lifeguard had to race over in his kayak and whack me repeatedly with his paddle to get me back on course. Apparently, I had inadvertently crossed the entire lake, straying hundreds of yards from the other participants.

It's slightly scary not to have the comfort of the wall I'm used to in the pool, but it's also liberating to be able to swim consistently, without having to stop and restart my momentum every twenty-five meters. With each tilt of my head out of the water to breathe, I feel more comfortable. Each stroke becomes smoother and faster as I'm able to shift my attention slightly away from meticulously analyzing my movements and more toward the bright sun shining down on my face and the tree-lined hills in the distance. By the time we reach the final orange buoy, before starting our second loop around the course, I recognize how happy I am that I chose to do the longest distance, that I don't yet have to get out of the water.

I surprise myself by only needing a couple of short breaks to catch my breath as the large "Finish" banner creeps closer and closer. *Maybe I am Michael Phelps,* I think to myself, momentarily remembering just how far I've come since those early days in the pool. With no one else remaining in the water but myself, Brita, and the antsy lifeguards (who are practically paddleboarding on my heels), a rush of adrenaline flows through me and suppresses the increasing hunger in my belly.

I bob my head out of the water, close enough to shore to make out dozens of swimmers and bystanders lined up by the finish line cheering me on. Justin and my other friends are wading into the water, preparing to help me out. I glance over at Brita, whose beaming smile overwhelms me with joy.

"Sweetie, you're nearly there! This is it! Finish it off!!"

I savor the last few strokes of the day as I charge toward the cheers and suddenly see my friends' legs under the water, which is now only a couple of feet deep.

The swim is over.

As they reach into the water and pull me out, I rip off my goggles and immediately search the shore for the large digital race clock, confirming that my competitive spirit is alive and well.

1 hour and 58 minutes.

While I hadn't set any strict expectations for time, I had estimated I would finish in three hours, or two and a half hours if I was very fast.

My friends carry me out of the lake and back onto land. Today, just this once, coming out of the freedom of the water and having to return to the confines of the wheelchair I hate so much is trumped by the tremendous sense of accomplishment and pride that swell up within me. It isn't just that I've completed the swim significantly faster than I expected. By having set and accomplished a goal that only six months ago seemed ridiculous and almost out of reach, I've renewed my faith in my ability to work toward my ultimate goal of getting back on my feet. Now that I've proven to myself that swimming more than a lap without a snorkel was simply a temporary obstacle—one that was ready to be overcome—working toward taking my first steps has become a tiny bit more achievable.

I bask in the warm sunshine and the sea of smiles and positivity that surround me as I speak the words out loud: "Let Michael Phelps be Michael Phelps. I… am… Aquaman!"

16.

Return to the Jedi

The rugged coastline and churning ocean look just as they did last winter when I was here. The tropical climate—with its regular rainstorms, year-round warm temperatures, and abundant sunshine—dictates that the scenery in Maui looks just as lush and vibrant in the summer as during the peak of winter. As I look out the window of the car, I see scores of paddleboarders and surfers in the water, battling through the powerful waves of this windswept north shore of the island.

In the months since I saw Alejandra last, I've worked hard to improve upon the neurological connections she helped establish in my body. When I came back home to California after that initial trip, I assumed I could take her suggestions, adapt them to the exercises and equipment I was using, and come up with a new and improved therapy plan that would implement her approach and result in me making gains much as I had in Maui. As it turned out, I was wrong.

My friends and family have repeatedly asked me what special sauce Alejandra provided. My trainers and physical therapists have been encouraged by my progress and intrigued to know more. "So, what kind of exercises does she do? How can we do them with you here?" they asked. My response generally was that the genius of Alejandra's innovative and unique method isn't something that can simply be added or applied to an existing regimen, especially since she uses Pilates equipment for our exercises. The inevitable response from whomever I've talked to was, "Oh great. There are lots of Pilates studios in the area! Can you go to these places?"

The reality is, I can't. It's not that simple. It's taken me months to realize this point, but now it's very clear. Alejandra's method isn't just the Pilates: it's not a matter of finding the same equipment, it's not a mental adjustment or a small variation in the exercises I'm doing already, and it has proven to be difficult to replicate. Her method is its own beast, one that is nearly impossible to explain or understand unless it is studied and felt in one's own body. And I've learned that the most important aspect of her method is the person behind it. Alejandra. Her understanding of spinal cord injury and her ability to diagnose and assess my neurological system's strengths and weaknesses are what has been missing since I left Maui. So it makes perfect sense that I've spent the last few months raising money and excitedly organizing another opportunity to come back to this magical island. And now here I am, driving back into the gravel driveway, seeing those same swaying palm trees and breathing in the gentle aromas of the tropical flowers and passionfruit vines that hug the walls next to her studio.

***

By the fourth day of my third week with Alejandra, I'm feeling more optimistic than I have on any day yet. The first two weeks were more challenging than I anticipated. Much to my dismay, I experienced no immediate revelations or significant changes. It took the better part of that time just for Alejandra to get reacquainted with my body—which has changed considerably—and for her to come up with a plan for how to tackle my many movement challenges and missing neurological connections. But yesterday was a huge breakthrough, and it couldn't have come any sooner because I was starting to experience some doubts about my ability to respond to Alejandra's method.

As on the preceding days, Alejandra got me into a standing position and practically hog tied me to the upright ladder of the Core Align (one of the standard pieces of Pilates equipment she uses), while she crouched and sandwiched herself in between my knees and the Core Align. Her two assistant trainers gripped my shoulders and hips to ensure I wouldn't tumble over. Following this complicated three-person setup, she started repeatedly sliding the moving carriage under one of my feet, hoping the recurring movement would establish a new neurological pathway to my legs.

Every day before this, I had completed the exercise exhausted, frustrated, and without success, but yesterday something clicked. Without realizing it, I started kicking the carriage back on my own. Alejandra noticed that she wasn't having to work as hard to manually move my foot back and forth, but it was only when she released her hand from the carriage completely and told me to look down that I acknowledged what was happening. Over and over, there I was, kicking my right leg backwards, initiating the movement through the pressure under my foot and extending my leg behind me, as if I were wiping off gum from the bottom of my shoe.

"Arash, you're doing it!" Alejandra practically screamed. "You're doing it all on your own!"

I went to sleep last night with a rare feeling of fulfillment and satisfaction, but today I'm a bit nervous. I'm worried that yesterday could have been a fluke and that I might not be able to replicate it. On top of that, Brita is arriving on Maui today—to relieve my friend Tony of his care-giving duties—and coming straight to the studio for my session. While I'm overjoyed at the prospect of sharing this breakthrough with her, I'm preparing myself for the possibility that my damaged and unpredictable body may continue to be… damaged and unpredictable, and I won't be able to show my girlfriend this incredible accomplishment.

As I swing the door open and enter the studio, Alejandra looks over at me animatedly and smiles as she greets me. "Arash! I'm so excited about yesterday! I hope you got some rest, because we're gonna keep working that same connection we established. I'm gonna work you so hard!" she says with glee as she cackles and helps me to begin our warm-up routine.

Thirty minutes into our session, I hear the crunch of tires in the driveway and know that Tony has returned from the airport with Brita. They walk into the studio, and Brita runs over to me, and without thinking, interrupts our exercise to embrace me. I happily oblige, yet I immediately feel more nervous about my imminent attempt to stand up and show her my breakthrough.

"Hi sweetie! I'm here! Did you miss me?" she says.

"You made it! I missed you so much. I'm so happy you're finally here!" I look over at Tony and wave. "No offense, bro."

"None taken," he responds with a smile. "She's way better looking than me anyways."

Brita sits down in the corner of the studio, as Alejandra and I jump back into our routine. After another hour and six more exercises—each targeting a different part of my body and helping me create a connection to those muscles—we make our way back to the Core Align. Alejandra's assistants come over, and we begin the arduous process of getting me up on my feet. We all nod in silent agreement, acknowledging the surprise we hope to unveil to Brita. Alejandra starts sliding the cart with my foot on it, and immediately I can feel that my body knows exactly what to do. I'm relieved. It only takes a few repetitions before I'm able to kick my foot and take control of the movement from Alejandra. She lifts one hand off the cart and loosens her grip on my other knee, then smiles at me and nods approvingly.

Brita is quietly typing on her laptop when I call out to her: "Brita, can you come take a look at this?"

"Of course. What's up?" she says as she walks casually over to the mess of four people and our intertwined and twisted limbs.

I glance at her without saying a word.

A few seconds later, she looks down at my feet and it hits her. "Are... *you* doing that?" she asks.

I smile and continue kicking.

"This is amazing! I can't believe this! You didn't tell me you could do this."

"It only started yesterday, and since I knew you were coming today, I figured I'd give you the full show. It's obvious my body was waiting for you to get here to allow a breakthrough like this," I say with a grin.

***

It's my last day on the island, and I'm wrapping up my final session with Alejandra before Brita and I leave for the airport. The last two weeks have been wonderful. Since my breakthrough on the Core Align, I've been able to improve and strengthen the newfound connection to my lower body every single day. My kicking has become stronger, and I stopped needing three people's help for me to stand. For the last several days, I've been able to do the same exercise with only Alejandra supporting me. Both of us have become more relaxed. I have stopped worrying that any movement while I'm upright may result in my tipping over like a falling tree, and she has realized there's no need for her to have a death grip on me for us to succeed.

After more than a month here, I'm thrilled about this breakthrough and my progress, yet I'm also nervous about continuing my recovery without having Alejandra's expertise every day. Never since my injury have I seen such a drastic improvement in such a short time. Until now, I've always had to work on a specific movement or exercise for weeks or months before I could notice an improvement. But here in this quiet little studio, on a small chunk of volcanic land in the middle of the Pacific Ocean, I've been able to notice a difference in my body consistently.

I again remember Grant's parting words for me before my first trip, and I attribute new meaning to them: "She is a *jedi*, bro..." Yes she is. I am convinced. I had no idea anyone could comprehend spinal cord injury on such a deep and complicated level, and Alejandra has blown me away. Now I have a much better understanding of Neurokinetic Pilates and why it has resonated so well with my body.

As I say goodbye, Alejandra gives me explicit instructions. "You have to do these exercises as much as possible, Arash," she says. "And it's very important to maintain the sequence of everything. You'll notice that what we do before I get you up standing has a deliberate order. That's important. You can't just jump up into standing first thing because your body and your neurological system won't be ready."

"You think I'll be able to get some similar results even though I won't be working with you and don't have access to the same equipment?" I ask.

She tightens her lips and looks at me stoically. I take her expression to be a confident recognition of the value of her expertise and method. "I don't know, honestly. But the good news is that we made the connection. It's there now. You just have to strengthen it."

"Yeah, I know. I'll do everything I can to do that. I just wonder how much stronger I could get if I stayed here longer."

Alejandra nods in agreement, smiles, and hugs us goodbye. We exit the studio and get into the rental car. As we make our way to the airport and head back to the mainland, I'm left to silently contemplate how I will manage to maintain this momentum of recovery.

17.

A Crazy Idea

It's only been a few days since I arrived back in California, yet somehow Maui already seems like a distant memory. From the moment I left her studio, I've set my sights on continuing the progress I made with Alejandra, retaining the neurological connection I made with my lower body, and becoming more confident doing exercises on my feet. I've continued rehab at my usual gym, and all of my trainers have acknowledged that something major has changed. Even in this short amount of time, I've noticed the ease with which I can raise myself to standing using parallel bars or a walker. Previously, I relied completely on my arms and upper body, but now I'm able to tap into that novel strength in my thighs and start to push through my skinny, soccer-player legs to get myself upright. I still need the walker or parallel bars for balance, but my legs have, in some ways, awoken.

On this Friday afternoon, as I make my way out of the gym—feeling satisfied after a good workout—I'm hit with a realization: the idea of standing independently, which seemed like an unattainable dream not long ago, now feels like a tantalizingly real possibility. I am quickly approaching the two-year anniversary of my injury, and despite all the negative prognoses I was given originally, I'm on the verge of achieving something monumental: standing up to my full height of six feet while supporting myself through the strength of my legs and using muscles I was told would never function again. Just as I finish that thought and put the key into the ignition to start my car, another idea pops into my head: *What if I could stand up, look at Brita eye-to-eye, and ask her to marry me?*

Although we've been together for two and a half years and developed a deeply committed relationship, Brita and I haven't had many explicit discussions about marriage. I want nothing more than to be with her and know that the daily challenges of this infuriating and debilitating injury will be significantly mitigated when I spend time with my best friend and "coolest person I've ever met," as I refer to her. My injury and the ensuing roller coaster ride of my recovery have put us through some of the most intense adversity any couple could face. Yet I still hold a deep fear that she might not want to spend the rest of her life with a person with so many needs—someone who can't yet go hiking with her or carry the groceries upstairs or easily provide her with the children and family I know she wants.

The few times I previously thought of proposing to Brita, I quickly abandoned the idea because I couldn't imagine getting down on one knee or proposing from a wheelchair. But now the opportunity to stand up on my own has opened the door to the possibility of this most unusual marriage proposal. Alejandra unmasked a dormant connection to my lower body on this recent trip, and not only did this reenergize my desire to accomplish what the surgeon told me was impossible, but it has now given me a new goal to commit to within my larger goal of recovery.

As I sit frozen in my car in the gym's parking lot, hand still holding the key in the ignition and eyes staring out the windshield, I know the decision has already been made. I may have only come up with this idea moments ago, but I know that it's too late to back out now. I will work as hard as I have to, and I will stand up and ask the woman of my dreams to marry me.

***

A couple of months have passed since that day in the car, and the summer seems to be going by quickly. While I've made gains in my attempts to strengthen my legs and stand, much as with every other aspect of my recovery, each step forward has been met with one step back. That's why I've kept my plan to stand up and propose to Brita a secret from my family and friends. I'm scared to tell them because I worry about the expectations that will be placed on me as a result, and I don't want to disappoint anyone, most of all myself.

I'm accustomed to the glacial pace of improvement and the up-and-down nature of my body's abilities, but I can't deny my growing frustration at the haphazard rhythm of my recovery. One day, my body feels connected, strong, and willing to be challenged. I make a small improvement or feel a muscle in my leg contract just a bit more strongly than before. The next day, all that may go away. I can try and try, and focus more than ever on being able to simply stand up and lock my legs out straight, but it won't seem to matter. My body will do what it wants to do, and I have no choice but to remain along for the ride and try to stay motivated.

***

It's the last week of August, and I just celebrated my thirty-third birthday. I am now well past the two-year mark of my injury, which is significant because that's when the doctors said the healing and improvements would surely stop. I never understood the idea that the body would have a ticking timer for healing, that my nerves and muscles and spinal cord and brain would somehow be motivated to repair themselves, but that after 104 weeks or 730 days had passed, it would all just stop. I didn't accept that idea back when I was in the hospital and I still don't accept it now. This explains why I've spent the last several weeks since the anniversary working harder than ever. I want to prove to myself—and everyone out there—that healing timelines are inaccurate, and that as long as one has the will to get better and the desire to work diligently toward that goal, there's no reason healing should stop.

Luckily, my extra effort has paid off. I completed some great days of rehab last week. For the first time, I was able to build on my accomplishments from one day to the next, and my trainers—who have seen a steady progression since my return from Maui—were giving me less and less support when I stood up. So it's no surprise that as I go into the gym today, I'm curious to see if I can keep the momentum going and continue my improvements with standing. Mondays always start off a bit slowly because I am coming back from the weekend. I'm rusty from two days of less activity, so I tame my expectations as my trainer takes me through the warm-up.

A couple of hours later, and after a number of exercises working my abs, hips, and legs, it's finally time to pull out the walker and assess my standing. I sit on the edge of the exercise table and breathe deeply to prepare.

"Okay, Arash, let's give it a shot and see where you're at today," says Lauren as she presses her palms against my knees to keep them stable.

"All right, here goes nothing." I brace my hands on the walker, push through my arms, and as I'm halfway up, my legs kick in and shoot me upright. My hips are under me, my knees are locked, and I'm standing very straight.

"Whoa, that's pretty strong! How do you feel?" asks Lauren.

"Actually... not bad... pretty good," I say through rapid breaths. The trainers used to have a death grip on my knees and strap two belts around my hips and attach them to the walker to keep me from wobbling and tumbling to my peril. Now, there are no straps or belts or complicated set ups. I am standing straight, on my own, for the first time in over two years.

Lauren slightly eases her pressure on my knees and looks up at me. "Arash, this is better than when we did it last week."

"Yeah I know. I like it! I think... you can take off your hands. I just want to try it and see."

"I think so, too. Here we go." She slowly removes her hands, but hovers them just inches from my knees, which are holding me upright. "That's all you! You got it!"

"Whoa, this feels good! Your hands are totally off, right?" I say with disbelief.

Lauren waves her hands in front of my face excitedly and smiles.

"This is great, I can't believe I'm—" But before I can finish my sentence, my knees buckle and I collapse back onto the table.

"Arash, that was awesome! I had my hands off completely for a few seconds. Nice work!"

I spend the remaining time trying to stand again. However, when Lauren takes her hands off now, while I'm able to maintain myself upright on my own, it never lasts more than a few seconds before I need to sit back down. Nevertheless, it confirms that the consistent improvements from last week—and in general since I came back from Maui—have resulted in something major, something that only a few months ago I didn't think was likely.

As I finish at the gym and make my way home, I still can't contain my excitement at the thought of what just happened, and what it means to the objectives I've been working toward. Even though I stood without assistance for only a few seconds, it was a significant breakthrough that I must continue to build upon and improve. I remember the phone call from Alejandra a few days ago telling me she is coming to Lake Tahoe in two weeks to teach a workshop about implementing her method for people with spinal cord injuries. She's asked me to come and provide a client's perspective for the attendees of the workshop. Tahoe is one of my favorite places, and only a few hours from my home, so I know I have to go. I wonder what her reaction will be when I show her I'm now able to stand up like this. Maybe by then I'll be able to stand for more than a few seconds. Maybe I can stand for a minute, or two, or ten! *Let's not get too far ahead of ourselves,* I tell myself as I realize that standing for that long is a crazy idea.

But then another crazy idea hits me: *What if I propose to Brita that weekend? What if I somehow organize a surprise and take advantage of this recent breakthrough with my body? What better place than Lake Tahoe, where I've gone skiing and camping my entire life, as a backdrop for this special moment?*

There is no doubt that this decision is hasty, impulsive, and risky because it gives me less than two weeks to improve my standing and plan the whole thing, but I decide to go for it wholeheartedly. As soon as I get home from the gym, I jump on the Internet and start furiously clicking through sites, looking for engagement rings. With a budget of nearly zero and no idea about what Brita might like, it feels a bit overwhelming. Then I suddenly remember a conversation in which she said something specific about jewelry: "I love peridot. I've always wanted a peridot ring." Both of us have August birthdays, which means peridot is our birthstone, so I take that as my cue and run with it. I find a beautiful ring online, but I also encounter two important obstacles: first, the ring will not arrive before I will have to leave for Alejandra's workshop, and second, I don't know what size would fit Brita's finger.

First, I call my friend Laura. I tell her my plan and demand that she and her boyfriend Justin come up for the weekend, and ask if I can have the ring shipped to her house. As my best friend since age nine, who has always supported me, she unhesitatingly accepts all of it.

One problem is solved, but my second challenge remains: how the hell do I guess the size of Brita's finger? Any sneaky idea I might come up with to measure it will be thwarted by the lack of time before I leave for Tahoe. The only thing I can think of is to consult with someone who might have a similar-sized hand and knows her finger measurement. I come up with a short list of names, but one person stands out from the rest. I call Jill, also one of my closest friends, because I know she won't be fazed by my request.

"Hey, what do you remember about Brita's hands?" I ask, skipping small talk and formalities.

"What? What are you talking about?"

I explain my plan, and after a solid laugh, she thinks about it and responds. "I think our sizes are probably pretty close. If anything, buy it a bit bigger, and you can always have it refitted later."

I breathe a sigh of relief, get back on my computer, and complete the order. It has all been decided and planned so quickly that I just now realize how excited I am. *This is happening! I don't know how or if I'll succeed, but I'm going to do it,* I tell myself. I contemplate telling my family and close friends about my intention, but decide that I'd rather keep it a surprise. My standing ability, though much improved, is still far from ideal, but something in me tells me to go for it. I've always listened to my gut and lived my life doing things when they *felt* right. When I stop and ask myself if my potential insanity is getting the better of me and if this all might be a terrible idea, there is no doubting voice within me, no declaration of hesitation or uncertainty. If nothing has spoken within me yet, then let it forever hold its peace, because I'm going for it!

Once the ring is ordered and the plan for Tahoe is set, I can't stop visualizing the moment over and over in my head. Every time I pull out the walker and practice getting myself up to standing, I imagine what it will be like in Tahoe. I visualize the crystal clear blue water of the lake, Brita's face, and the surrounding mountains, and I hope more than anything that this crazy idea will somehow work out.

18.

Stand and Deliver

I slow down the car as we approach the winding curves and narrow switchbacks descending into Emerald Bay, where for one brief stretch, the lake is visible on both the left and the right. Its rich, deep blue water matches the cloudless sky, as it welcomes the bright shimmer of the warm Sierra Mountain sunlight.

"We used to always come to this area of Lake Tahoe with my parents when I was a kid," I tell Brita. "When I think back, although part of me wishes I could have traveled abroad as a child and gone on fancy trips to London or Rome, as some friends were doing, I'm actually happy our summer vacations consisted of these camping trips to the mountains, to this amazing place. It's what planted the seed in me to love the outdoors and be excited to get out into nature. Now, I wouldn't change a thing."

"That's crazy, because this is an area of the lake I didn't come to much when I lived here," Brita responds. "I'm excited we're spending the weekend here and I get to see this park you know so well. What's it called, again?"

"D.L. Bliss State Park. It's gorgeous. We're almost there now."

Sometimes I forget that for a year and a half, Brita lived in Lake Tahoe, amidst the ski bums and mountain adventurers. She wasn't just one of the many who drove four hours to ski and snowboard in the winter or engage in outdoors activities in the summer, and then went home to the Bay Area; she lived here full time. I love that Brita is so adaptable and open to new experiences, that the third-born child from a Minneapolis suburb was as comfortable spending years abroad—much of it in the heart of Paris—as she was moving to the small mountain community in Tahoe. Her easygoing nature and desire to explore the world are two of her many qualities I fell in love with early on.

It's the second week of September and the summertime crowds have dwindled, so when we arrive at the park, we have our choice of campgrounds to accommodate our group of friends.

"When is everyone else getting here?" Brita asks.

"They should be here before dark. Want to go down to the water? There's a great sandy beach area. We can brainstorm our campfire dinner there," I say with a smile.

"Sounds great."

After we park the car and I'm waiting for Brita to grab the wheelchair from the trunk of the beat-up Subaru, I sneakily peek at my phone to see the text I've been expecting from Laura.

Got the wine and supplies. We're driving up now. And I didn't forget the special little box! Can't wait for this all to go down. See you soon!

***

Our friends have joined Brita and me around the campfire at our campsite and it feels like any other camping trip with friends. Night is falling slowly, and the eight of us have just finished dinner and are chatting jovially and enjoying the crystal clear sky, which is filling with stars by the minute. Brita gets up to walk over to the restroom, and immediately, as if a silent alarm has rung, my friends huddle around.

"Okay, so where are you going to do it tomorrow?" Laura asks.

I glance over to make sure Brita has entered the bathroom, then whisper, "I'm not sure, but I have a couple of ideas. The beach here in the state park is pretty nice, although the sand is always a challenge with the wheelchair. I guess I'll have to see how close I can get to the water without going through the sand."

Dave, an Irishman who has spent the last decade in San Francisco, and with whom I've been on many backpacking trips in the past, leans into the group. "What about somewhere else close by, outside the park?" He swings his head around and surveys the area, as if he can assess the surroundings through the dark silhouettes of the trees and blackness.

"I'm all ears, guys. Any ideas are welcome." I see the bathroom door swing open in the distance. "Okay, she's coming back. Just gotta keep the secret for one more day!"

Without missing a beat, Dave launches into a random story, which he makes sound fully convincing when Brita sits back down at the campfire.

***

The next morning, I struggle to make the difficult transfer from sitting on the ground inside the tent to sitting in the wheelchair, which is still cold from the overnight mountain air. Before I can start to push myself through the dirt and toward the picnic table, Justin—Laura's boyfriend, who pushed me energetically down to the lake for the 2.4-mile swim— runs over to me and crouches down on one knee. "Bro, I went for recon this morning. I know where you're going to do it."

"Really?" I say, slightly skeptical of his confidence. "Did you find a good spot at the beach?"

He looks at me intensely, unable to hide his genuine excitement, and shakes his head. "Even better. It's just up the road. Have you been to Sugar Pine Point Park?"

I dig through my memory, but come up with nothing. "You think it's good?"

He smiles. "It couldn't be better. We can easily park the car and go down a paved path to a beautiful pier right on the lake. It's seriously the perfect spot. Do you trust me?"

"Of course." I smile back, relieved and simultaneously exhilarated at the thought that the biggest moment in my relationship with Brita is about to occur.

***

We are getting ready to drive to the park. The moment is getting closer and closer, but I'm not nervous. It all feels so right, so natural, so matter of fact—and as such, I'm surprisingly calm, even though I have no idea if or how my body will cooperate with me.

When Laura casually brought up the idea that we all go over to the park and check out the view of the lake, Brita admitted she had never been and that it would be a great plan for the late afternoon. Now, with their quick winks and subtle thumbs-up indicating to me that some element of the plan is in order, my friends are doing a great job of keeping the secret from Brita, yet I'm still worried she'll be able to sniff us out somehow.

We arrive at the park and get out of our cars. As Brita is grabbing my wheelchair from the trunk, I ask her to also bring the walker. We've recently been keeping it in the car at all times because I don't like to practice standing in public, so I quickly say something to diffuse any possible suspicion. "You always say you want me to practice standing more often, so this is a good chance, right? With a view of the lake and all?"

"Yes! That's great. I'm so happy you said that. I'll grab it!"

I smile with glee. A couple of friends look over at me, desperately trying to hide their beaming grins. They are smiling so obviously that I worry they may give something away. I keep Brita in conversation, pushing the wheelchair as fast as I can so the two of us stay ahead of the rest of the group. I hope she won't notice the clinking of the bottles and the oversized backpacks they're carrying as they follow behind us. I see the pier now in the distance, and just as Justin said this morning, it's perfect. But as we get closer, I notice dozens of well-dressed people crowding the pier, chatting, and enjoying the view. And there are chairs set up for a wedding ceremony on the hill above the pier.

Of course... of course there's a wedding right now! I think to myself.

But just as I start to worry about sharing my special moment with fifty-seven strangers on a narrow little pier, the wedding guests suddenly turn away from the lake and begin walking off the pier. They must have been given a signal that the ceremony was starting, because within seconds, they are all gone and the pier is nearly empty. Even though I'm not a religious person, I glance up at the sky and thank the higher powers that just made this magic happen.

"This is so cool! I'm glad we came here," Brita says with a smile.

"Maybe we can go out on the pier, and I can practice standing there with the walker. I'll try my best not to fall into the water," I say with a snicker.

"Um… Okay! If you feel comfortable, then let's do it!"

I turn around and face the rest of my friends. Thankfully, Brita still hasn't noticed the inordinate amount of gear they're carrying. "Hey, we're just going to take a quick wander down to the end of the pier," I tell them.

They flash knowing smiles and quickly shuffle past us toward a picnic table overlooking the pier. Justin mentioned that specific table to me this morning, saying that it was the ideal place for them to set up the wine, food, and everything we needed for the festivities, while still keeping an eye on Brita and me. It just so happens that no one is occupying it. I thank the universe, higher powers, or gods again.

Before she can realize that our friends have walked past us without saying a word, I take Brita's hand and nudge her forward on the pier. The conditions can't be more perfect. The afternoon sun has begun its slow descent toward the peaks of the high mountains, and the calm waters of the lake reflect a serenity and harmony that are a welcome reprieve to my steadily increasing heart rate.

"How's this?" I say. "I can stand up here."

Dave told me he would capture the moment with his fancy camera and zoom lens, so I turn the wheelchair at a slightly awkward angle to make sure we're facing the picnic table where our friends have now settled. Like birds scattered throughout a tree's branches, they're all sitting separately and quietly. Although we're too far away to see their expressions, I can tell they're doing their best to guard the secret for another few minutes.

I slap my right hand on my front pocket one last time to confirm the ring is there before I grab both handles of the walker and get ready to stand. I take a deep breath, think of everything that has happened in the last few months to get me here—to this day, this place, and this precise moment. I think about the overwhelming joy I feel at every second I spend with Brita, and how certain I am about my decision. It feels like everything has lined up just the way I wanted, and for what it's worth, even the universe has my back. I give one more silent acknowledgment of gratitude to the higher powers, before I push myself up to standing.

At first, my legs are like jelly. It feels as if I'm trying to stand atop two shaky noodles. I hold my body weight through my arms as I try to will my legs to engage and cooperate with me. But it's no use. After thirty seconds of wobbles and two tired arms, I flop back into the wheelchair in frustration.

Brita anticipates my reaction and tries to immediately comfort me. "It's okay, sweetie. Don't get upset. You can always try again later."

You have no idea what's about to happen! I want to say to her. *There is no way this can be tried again later. It's now or next summer or never. This. Must. Happen. Now.*

I push myself up to standing again. And this time everything connects. My legs immediately straighten, my knees lock out, my hips stay solidly under me, and I'm eye-to-eye with Brita.

"Looking good!" she says. "I'm glad you're taking my advice to practice standing more, even if it's out in public."

"Yeah I guess you're right," I mutter as I focus on keeping myself upright.

Knowing that I'm naturally inclined to improvise and speak straight from the heart, I haven't planned or written anything specific to say. I look around at the scenery and think of a flowery, cheesy introduction to the big moment. I come up with nothing of substance, nothing better than some generic fluff out of an Adam Sandler romantic comedy. I scrap the idea as I realize I have no idea how long my standing will last. My legs could potentially give out on me in the next ten or thirty or sixty seconds. There's no time to lose.

I let the walker go with my right hand—anxiously hoping my left arm can support my unsteady upper body—and reach into my pocket. As I pull out the ring box, I realize I don't have the finger dexterity to flip it open with one hand. I stare at it for a second and contemplate what to do, while Brita is facing away from me, looking out at the lake. This is probably as good as it's going to get, so I decide there's no turning back now. I tap Brita on the shoulder, hoping she'll notice what I'm holding. But she doesn't look down.

Instead she looks right at me. "What is it, sweetie?"

I nudge her with my free elbow, sway a little bit, and hold up the ring box. "Will you marry me?"

She looks at me and smiles incredulously for what feels like an eternity. "What? Are you serious?"

"Yes, of course!" Both my hands are back on the walker, and my legs are struggling. I conjure up every bit of energy and endurance I can muster to stay standing. "So... will you? Will you marry me?"

"Really?" She places her hand gently on my shoulder, which for my amateur standing abilities feels like she's put a forty-pound weight on me. "This is so much sooner than I was expecting. I figured this wouldn't happen for another year or two, so you could have more time to work on your recovery."

I try to tighten every muscle I can, and my body responds. I've bought myself a few more precious seconds of remaining upright. "So does that mean yes?!" I say with more than a hint of impatience. "I'm not exactly sure how long I can keep this up while you decide."

She smiles more broadly than I've ever seen her smile, and cradles my face. "Oh! Of course, baby! Of course I will! You know I will!"

"I mean I figured… but I had to get the official response from you!" My left knee unlocks, and I lose my balance for a second, but I'm able to straighten the knee again and stay upright.

"I can't believe it! I can't believe you did this now… like this… standing up! You're amazing!" she says with glee, then kisses me.

"I haven't stopped thinking about this for months, and I'm just as surprised as you that I'm still standing! I love you so much. I've only gotten this far because of you and everything you do for me. I can't imagine a day without you."

What ensues are a couple of the calmest and happiest minutes of my life. A friendly couple paddle by in a kayak and congratulate us when we tell them we just got engaged. I look back at my friends and can feel, if not see, their radiant smiles. Dave is making his way slowly toward the pier, his face hiding behind the massive zoom lens of his camera, as he leans this way and that, trying for the perfect photo.

Brita and I remain standing, holding hands, kissing, exchanging smiles. Thankfully, I'm not thinking about my legs as they are somehow staying locked and straight without me having to make any effort. For the first time since I fell off that balcony and shattered my neck over two years ago, there is no struggle, no fight. I am numb to the constant resentment, frustration, and anger I have felt for having to go through this horrific injury. I'm not thinking about the consistent and overwhelming pain of living in a body that feels everything but can't yet respond to my commands—a situation that used to seem unthinkable, but is now an all-too-normal aspect of my daily life. I'm not thinking about the pervasive physical discomfort I endure every single day from having to sit so much. And right now, as I'm standing up, even the wheelchair, which I simultaneously loathe yet recognize for its necessity, is behind and below me. It's not touching my body and it's not affecting my perspective on the world. It's a non-factor, as I always want it to be.

For just these few moments, I'm consumed with the beauty of this world, of *my* world. Of the mountains that I explored and gallivanted in as a child, and that surround me now. Of the smiles and support of my family and friends that have enveloped me for the last two years, giving me strength to know I can continue forward. Of remembering that I was lying on that cold concrete two years ago, body shattered and just as close to leaving this world forever as I was to taking another breath to survive, and of knowing that for whatever reason, I was given a ticket to live.

Right now, for this moment here with Brita, it feels as if time has stood still. And while part of me wishes it would—that I could remain here forever, standing, embracing the love of my life and numb to the pain I have become all too accustomed to—I know my work is not yet done, the final chapter has not yet been written, and I must continue on my path and live the only way I know to live: with enduring passion, unlimited gratitude, unwavering commitment, and undying love.

Epilogue

Standing up to propose to Brita was an unforgettable, momentous, and immensely satisfying accomplishment. But as I've shared in the preceding chapters, my primary objective has always been to relearn to take steps, so my story doesn't conclude with the proposal. I've remained on my path to regain as much function as possible, improve my quality of life, and continue my activism and support for changing how the medical system deals with spinal cord injuries, and I have a number of significant updates you may find relevant and interesting. In addition, I want to share some of the questions I am most frequently asked and my responses, as well as potential takeaways I hope can contribute to your perspective and life.

***

Shortly after that magical experience in Lake Tahoe, I shared my proposal on my blog. An acquaintance I had not seen in years asked if I would tell my story at a conference he was organizing. He wanted a TED-style talk—genuine and personal, but appealing to a general audience. I agreed, assuming it would be a small gathering of his professional peers and a fun opportunity to share my story. The next thing I knew, I was on a conference some of the most successful venture capitalists and CEOs in Silicon Valley. The presentation was a success, and thanks to the generous support and outreach of my friends—especially one I will refer to only as Irish Dave because I know he prefers to remain humble and mysterious—I started getting more invitations to speak to a variety of audiences and events.

Exactly one year after I wobbled onto my feet to propose to Brita, I met the standing ovation of seven hundred cheering people by standing up confidently to conclude my speech. After my TEDx talk began to spread online, I got even more offers to share my story. I have spoken in large auditoriums, small company off-sites, storytelling open mic nights in cafés, executive meetings, conferences, and universities. One audience—the group I felt could benefit the most from my perspectives—was future doctors and surgeons as they completed their coursework on neurological conditions in medical school. I have discovered tremendous pleasure in sharing my perspectives and lessons from living through this unimaginable life change and persevering through continued challenges and adversity. To this day, I have never turned down an invitation to share my experiences.

Beyond my personal story, I've always wanted to have a larger impact and help others like me who have dealt with the trauma of a life-changing illness or injury. My frustrations with the pervasive negative and outdated approaches of the medical system created a profound desire within me to actively make a change. In 2015, I teamed up with three exceptionally talented, forward-thinking, and like-minded physical therapists and neurological specialists, and we co-founded the No Limits Collaborative. The mission of this California-based 501c3 nonprofit is to improve the quality of life for individuals with spinal cord injuries and neurological conditions by providing access to physical therapy, rehabilitative services, and wellness programs, through advocacy, research, and education. Some of our accomplishments so far include providing personalized physical therapy and rehab sessions; facilitating educational workshops and presentations; organizing mixed-ability (people with and without disabilities) relay teams to participate in triathlons, swims, and athletic events; and developing and implementing a comprehensive model for exercise and fitness for disabled students and faculty at UC Berkeley.

I continue to dedicate a large portion of my time to my physical therapy, rehabilitation, and recovery. While I'm not yet able to take steps, I have become increasingly comfortable standing for long periods of time with the help of a walker. Progress is painfully slow and sometimes seemingly unnoticeable, but I continue to work hard toward my ultimate objective. In my rehab, I regularly spend one to two hours per day doing exercises standing up and on my feet to slowly strengthen the nascent but improving muscles and body parts.

Although I have tried a variety of conventional and alternative exercise and rehab methodologies, practitioners, gyms, therapy centers, and approaches in my quest to regain function throughout my body, by far the most successful method has been the Neurokinetic Pilates work I did with Alejandra Monsalve (see chapters 13 and 16). I have gone back to visit

Alejandra a couple more times to reassess my physical abilities and continue finding more ways to create new neurological connections within my body. Thankfully, my physical therapists and trainers at home have been very open minded and adopted Alejandra's exercises and methods in my continued work with them.

Because my medical insurance cut me off from *all* physical therapy only four months after my injury and repeatedly denied my requests and appeals for continued exercise and care, I've been forced to come up with a variety of creative fundraising efforts to enable me to continue my treatments and physical therapy. One of these is Comedy For a Spinal Cause (CFASC), which began as a one-time fundraiser for my recovery and turned into an effort with much greater scope and impact. In 2013, Irish Dave organized a standup comedy event where he asked an old roommate—now a successful comedian in Los Angeles—to donate his comedic efforts for a charitable cause. Two other comedians joined in, local companies donated beer and wine, and more than one hundred and fifty people showed up on a Wednesday night to a funky event space in San Francisco. We raised more than $6,000 for my recovery.

Many people told us how much they enjoyed that event and asked when we would have another. We seized this opportunity and decided to repeat the comedy show six more times over the next three years. Each event was committed to a different local person with a spinal cord injury, with all proceeds going to his or her recovery efforts. Now, comedians were coming to us and asking if they could participate at the next show! Our most recent

CFASC event sold out quickly, with almost two hundred and fifty attendees and seven of the best local headlining comedians. As excited I am about this accomplishment, I continue to look for other innovative opportunities to help people in my community get access to the funds they so desperately need for a better quality of life.

As I described in chapter 15, swimming and water exercises have grown to be a more significant part of my recovery efforts, overall health and fitness, and everyday well-being. After I completed the 2.4-mile swim, I looked for a longer, more challenging swim competition, but to no avail. That's when I decided to create my own event. Following a visit with friends and a casual weekend swim in Donner Lake—a few miles down the road from the frigid waters of Lake Tahoe—I decided I would circumnavigate the lake and more than double my previous accomplishment.

It seemed slightly insane to consider swimming five miles in a sixty-eight-degree lake at a six-thousand-foot elevation, but I decided to commit myself to this goal within my larger goal of recovery. I invited anyone interested in challenging his or her own respective limits and boundaries to participate, and I dedicated the event to our nonprofit by turning it into a high-profile fundraiser. After eights months of training, organizing, and planning, I was joined by forty-five other swimmers and more than one hundred friends, family members, and supporters as we turned a quiet Saturday morning in September into the Donner Party Swim. After four hours and twenty-nine minutes of swimming, I came out of the lake with dizzy eyes and chattering teeth, but immensely proud of accomplishing this seemingly impossible feat.

***

Whenever I talk about my injury and recovery—be it with friends, family, or in an interview or formal speaking event—I am often asked the same questions. I want to share my responses to these questions here to provide additional perspective and guidance for readers.

Q: Have you gotten used to the wheelchair?

A: Absolutely not. I'm sorry if that's not what people want to hear, but it's the truth. Because I have sensation throughout my entire body—even in those parts I can't move very well—sitting in a wheelchair causes immense pain and discomfort every day. As a result, I have to plan out each day to minimize the time I spend sitting and to manage my pain. When I'm at home, I spend as little time in the wheelchair as possible, preferring to lie flat to write, read, or work on my computer. I keep a walker in the car at all times so I can stand up easily wherever I might be.

I've always hated the reality of being two feet shorter than everyone around me, and unfortunately, I haven't become accustomed to that, even after all this time. I'm a social person and used to love parties, large gatherings, concerts, and events with many people. Now, those situations usually make me uncomfortable, and I'm very selective when it comes to putting myself into situations with large crowds and with many people standing all around me, who often do not notice me or bump into me.

Additionally, I do not like constantly assessing the accessibility of wherever I go. I live in an area where most of my friends and family live in old buildings, and rarely do I have safe and easy access to enter their homes. I feel lucky that because of the Americans with Disabilities Act, *most* restaurants, stores, hotels, and public and government buildings (with *many* exceptions) are wheelchair accessible. While this is helpful for meeting people in public or performing basic tasks and errands, I get impatient and annoyed with having to call places in advance to confirm accessibility, especially when I'm traveling. Sometimes places say they are accessible but they're not. Other times, people don't even know how to answer my questions and prefer to say they can't accommodate me, in order to protect themselves from liability. This continues to be a point of frustration to me, but because I don't want to be stuck at home all the time, I choose to get out into the world and do my best to deal with the wheelchair challenges.

Q: Do you think there will be a cure for paralysis or spinal cord injury soon?

A: I hope so, but I have no idea and I don't think about it very much. I keep up with the most recent research, but I don't hold out hope that there will be an easy solution or cure anytime soon. Even if a cure—or the term I prefer is a *very effective treatment*— were to be discovered, it would take a long time for it to get tested and approved by all the different medical and governmental agencies and organizations to ensure safety and efficacy. So I'm not holding my breath for something to happen in the near future. Additionally, a body that has suffered the trauma of major damage to the spinal cord will need time and great effort to respond to any external treatment, even if it is effective. When better treatments become available, I will celebrate and hopefully partake in them, but in the meantime, I will continue my efforts to strengthen and improve my body and regain as much function as possible.

Q: How do you decide which therapies and treatments to try?

A: I have kept an open mind from the beginning. Maybe because the primary attitude of the doctors and physical therapists I encountered was so negative and discouraging, I always believed there had to be other treatments out there that could help. It was very difficult when I first came home from the hospital and had little information or guidance, but with the help of other people with spinal cord injuries, as well as countless hours of reading and Internet research, I began to find opportunities. I've tried a number of different therapies and treatments, but I haven't said yes to everything. Sadly, some people and companies take advantage of individuals who are dealing with these injuries and who are in an extremely vulnerable time, and promise them great results. I think there is a balance between being open minded and maintaining a discerning and skeptical eye.

My advice is to consider how specific and individual your experience is when it comes to spinal cord injuries or neurological conditions. I haven't found treatments that work for everyone. Each injury is too unique and has a different impact. Ten people can have the same classification for their injuries or have broken the identical vertebrae, yet they can have ten completely different outcomes. I've seen this with my own eyes!

I suggest always having an honest conversation and dialogue with your body and see how it feels with any treatment of exercise. This isn't as strange or ambiguous as it may sound; I simply mean to have full faith in what your body is telling you, and don't be afraid to make changes or try new things. I tried certain treatments in the past that worked for me, but then they no longer helped, so I stopped them. There's no reason to waste your time and money doing something if you don't feel it's helping you. Trust yourself and listen to your body. No one knows what it really feels like but you, so let that guide you and your decisions. Ask questions, do lots of research, and don't take any one person's or organization's word as an absolute truth. Trust your sensations and instincts; surround yourself with people who believe in and support you; and be committed, diligent, and patient.

Q: Have you found a way to enjoy the same things you did before your injury?

A: Yes and no. Obviously, almost everything athletic that I used to do is not feasible anymore. I can't play soccer or run or go on a hike in the mountains. Nothing can replace that. I explained my relationship to swimming at length in chapter 15, and this has become my exercise of choice. I absolutely love it! It's the only activity that gives me the same physical satisfaction that other activities did before my injury.

Additionally, I've played music my entire life: violin and clarinet when I was a child, and guitar from my teenage years until the day of my injury. Although I'm extremely lucky to have decent strength in my hands (usually cervical injuries result in very limited finger, hand, and wrist function), I'm not able to play guitar very well anymore. This has proven to be a sensitive and frustrating subject for me because I greatly miss being able to play music and having that creative outlet.

That said, I did regain enough strength in my hands and fingers to cook, which has been a strong passion of mine since I was nine. As soon as I was able to start holding a knife and chopping an onion—albeit, very slowly and sloppily at the beginning—I cooked as much as possible. It was great to have a goal-oriented task that was simultaneously improving my hands and also satisfying a deeper part of my personality. I suppose much of the energy and time I used to spend doing physical activities and playing music has been channeled into cooking. This has made me much more skilled in the kitchen because I'm constantly challenging myself in new ways and finding great joy in sharing my food with others.

Q: How do you continue to stay motivated, even after all this time?

A: That's easy. I want nothing more than to walk. I'm slightly obsessed. I think about it all the time, I visualize it, I dream about it nearly every night. As long as I have the intense desire to get back on my feet and to move without the need of a wheelchair, I can motivate myself to work toward my goal. And so I continue on my path.

***

I continue to share my story through speaking events and through blogging on my website. If you'd like to get in touch with me or see my latest updates, feel free to check it out at https://arashrecovery.com

Made in the USA
San Bernardino, CA
30 September 2017